Art Studio Model

Michiru North

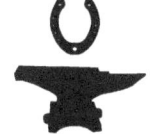

Merry Blacksmith Studio

2015

Art Studio Model: Michiru North

Merry Blacksmith Studio
70 Lenox Ave.
West Warwick, RI 02893

merryblacksmith.com
merryblacksmithstudio.com
merryblacksmithshop.com

Published in the USA by The Merry Blacksmith Studio

ISBN—1-51521-406-0
978-1-51521-406-9

Art Studio Model: Michiru North

Introduction
(or, What This Book Is and How To Use It)

The Art Studio Model series is aimed at artists of all levels—from beginner to advanced—and is meant to serve as both a reference and a source of inspiration.

To us, the human figure is one of the most fascinating and, dare we say, enjoyable subjects to draw, paint, and sculpt. This series will feature a variety of types of models as it progresses. This particular volume features model Michiru North. We find her a fun model to work with and there may be more volumes featuring her in the future.

We feature models in classic modeling poses from various different angles, set from the height of an artist standing at their easel. In this volume, we've played a little bit with the late in some instances in order to cast some interesting shadows here and there. We've seen plenty of model reference books around. What makes us different is that we try to keep things interesting.

As for how to use this book, we have a few suggestions. We favor cookbook stands to keep the pages open to our current project. It's with that idea in mind that we made sure that there was a lot of room between the subject image and the binding. (That space is also useful to jot down notes.)

Other suggestions would be to go ahead and break the binding by pressing the pages open against a flat surface. You could cut the pages out and tape them next to your easel. It's your book. You can do whatever you'd like to it. We know one woman who took her copy to the local copy shop, had the binding trimmed off and replaced with a spiral binding. We thought of offering the book to you that way, but we also wanted to keep the cost down. (Hey, we're artists too. We know how important keeping to budget is.)

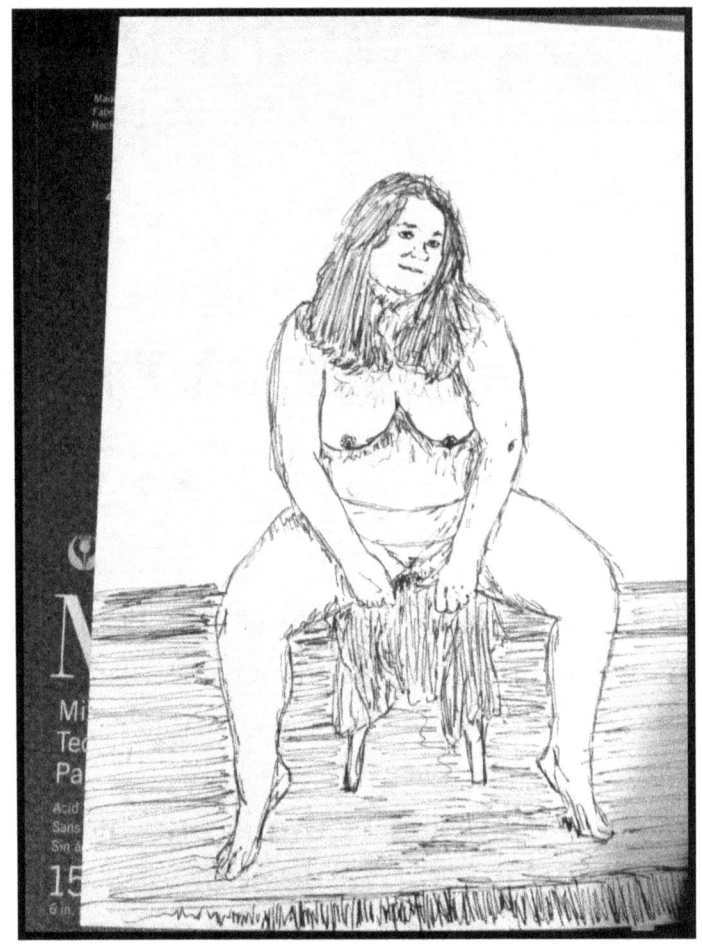

Quick pen sketch of Image 40.

With all of that in mind, please enjoy this book. We hope you find it useful and inspirational. And don't forget to look for other books in this series.

Cheers!

– The Merry Blacksmith Studio

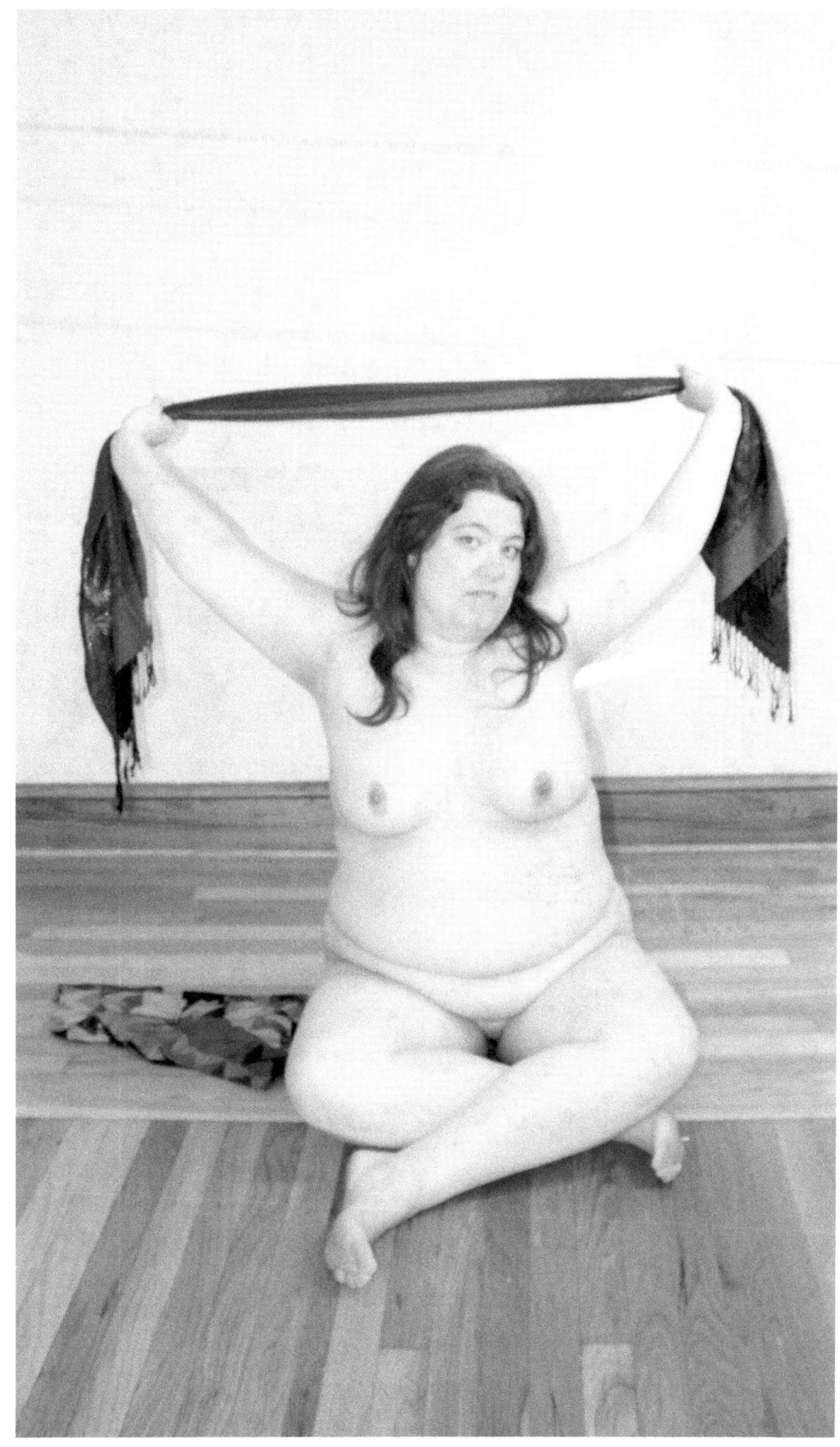

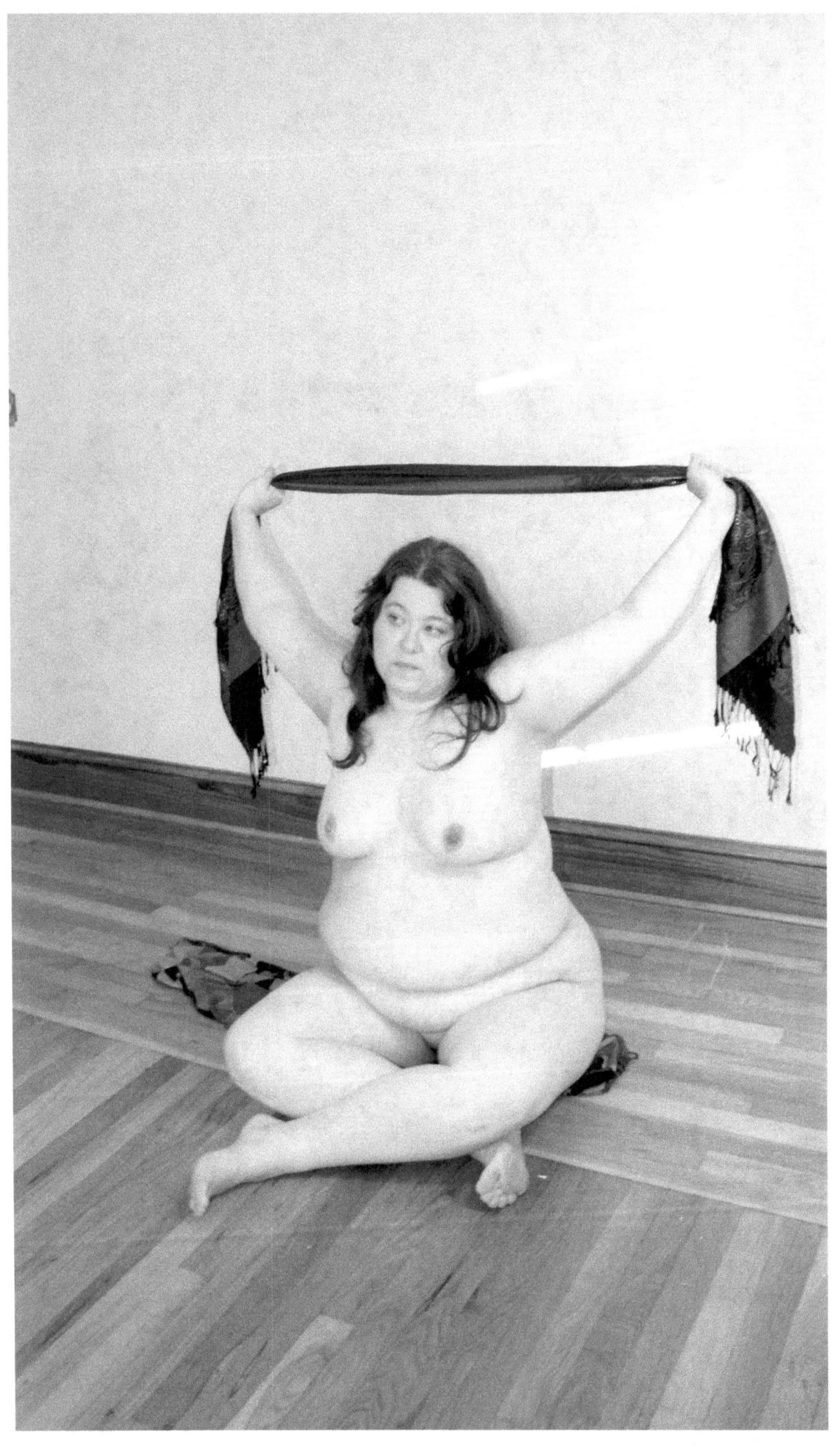

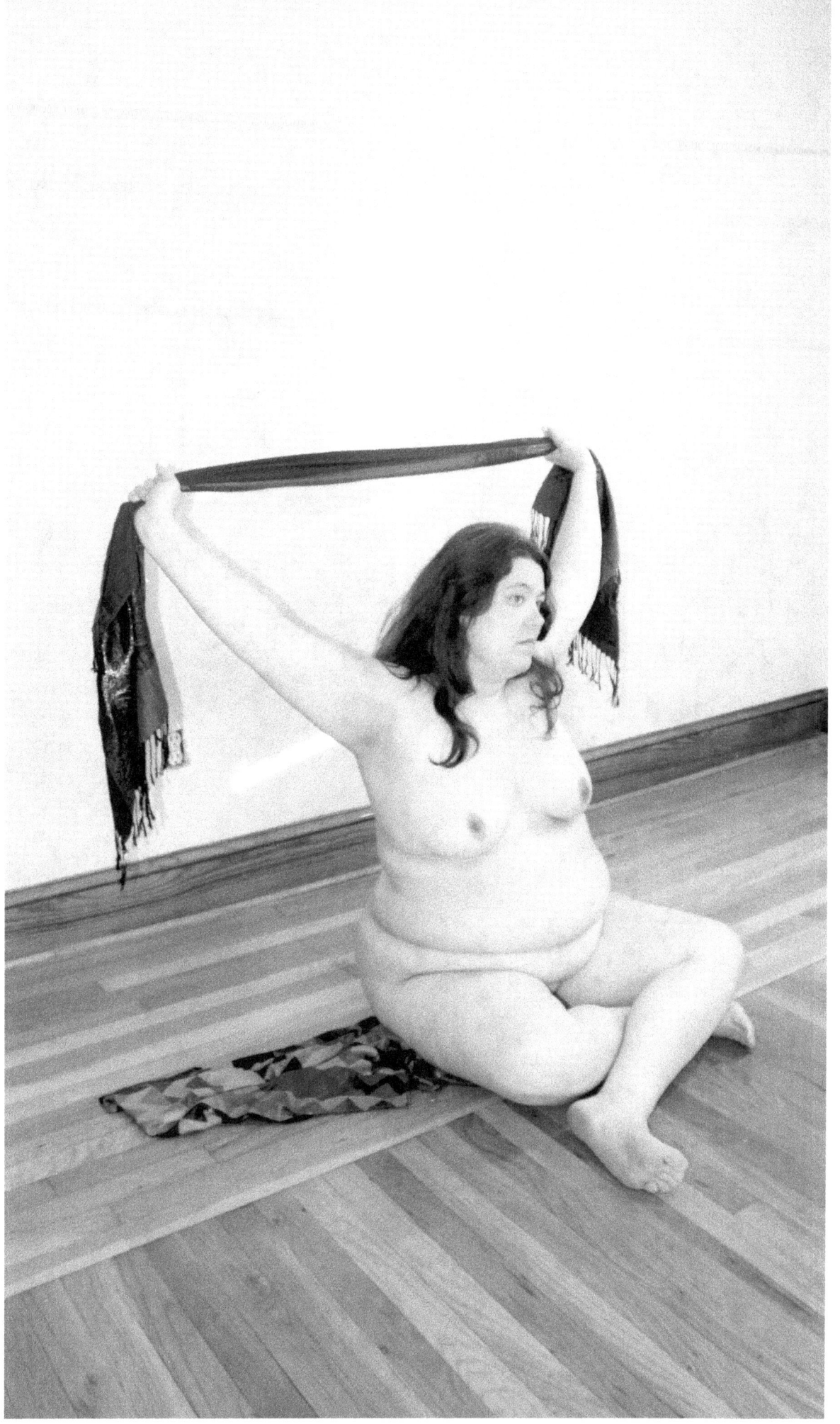

3

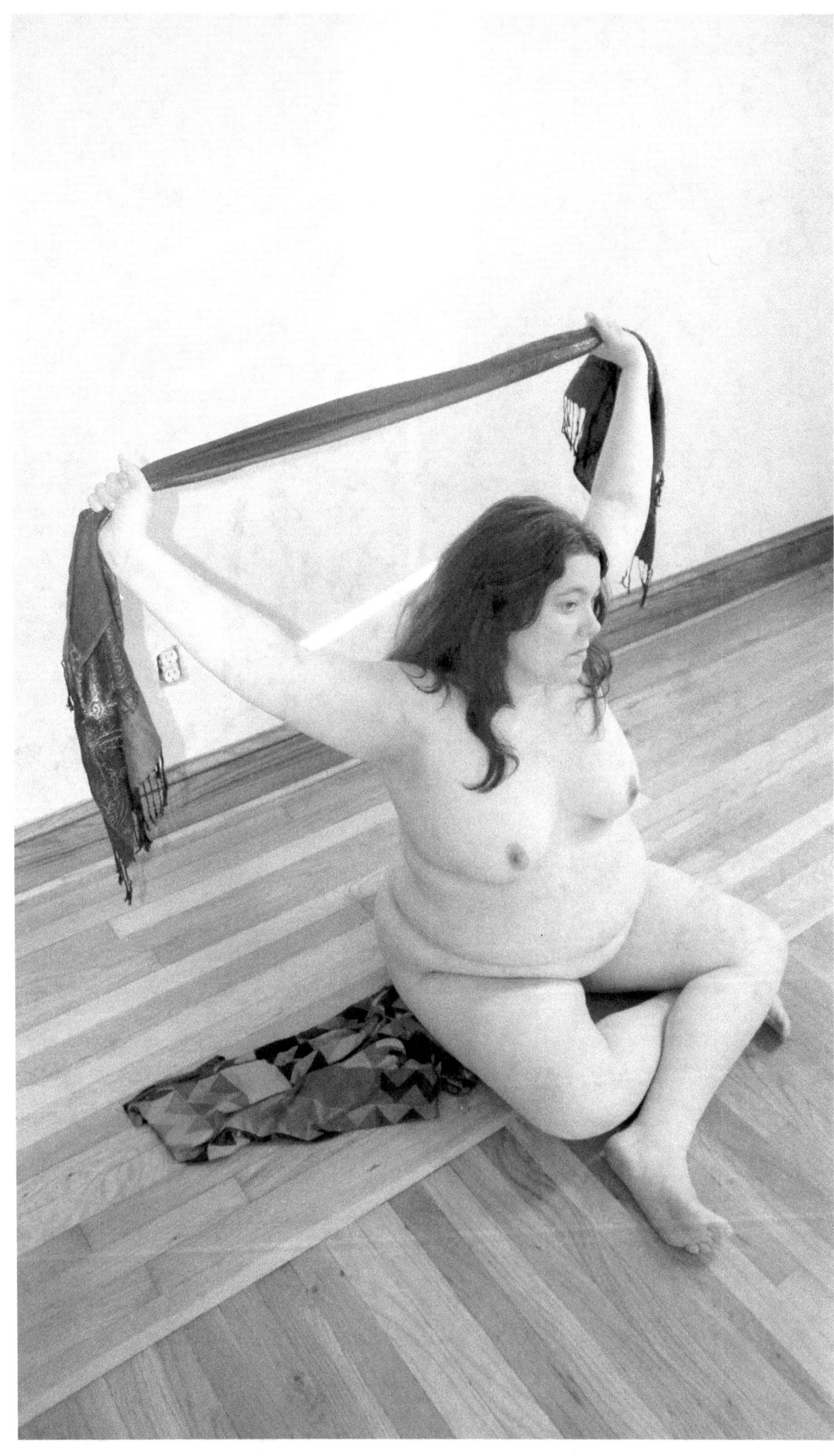

4

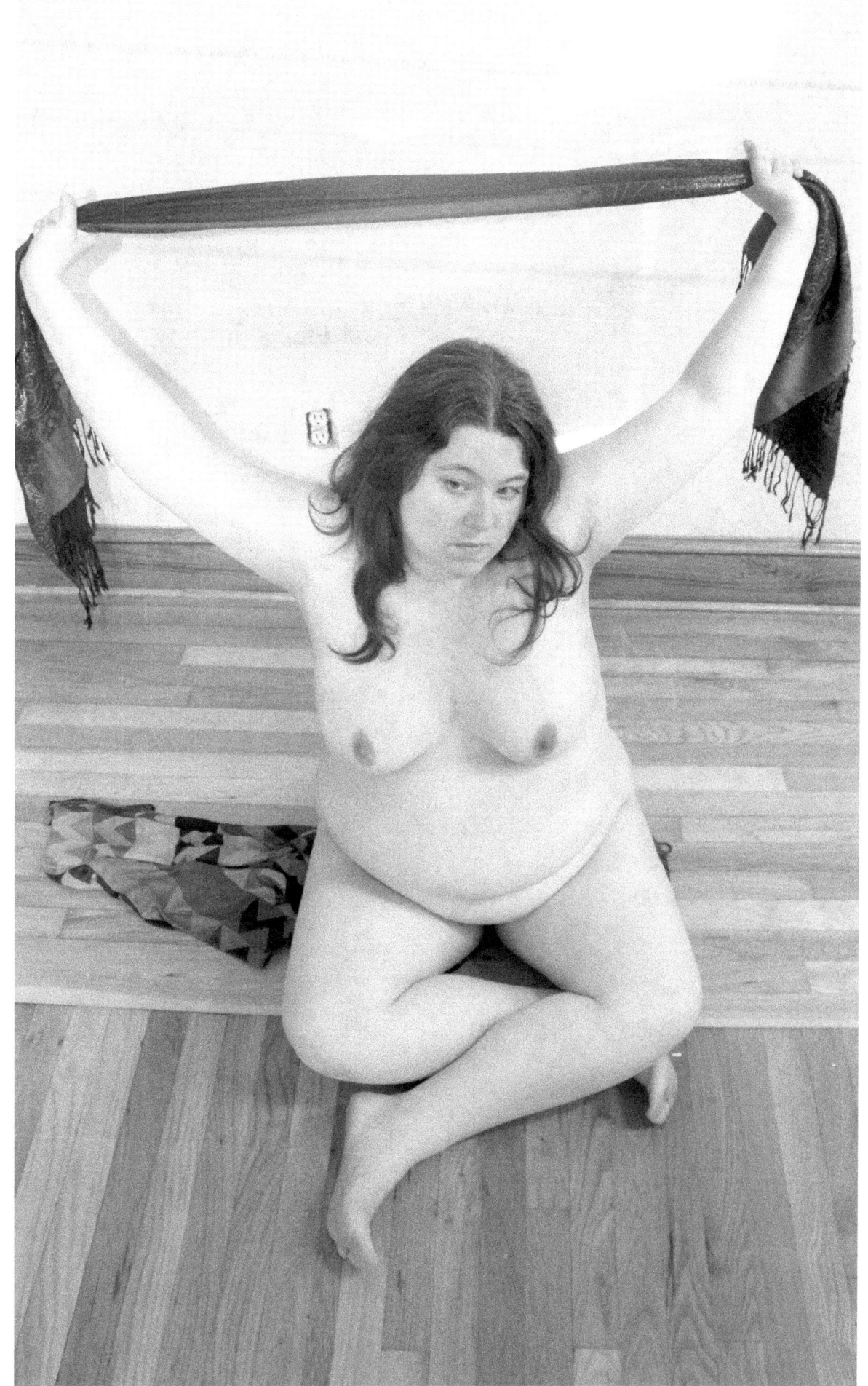

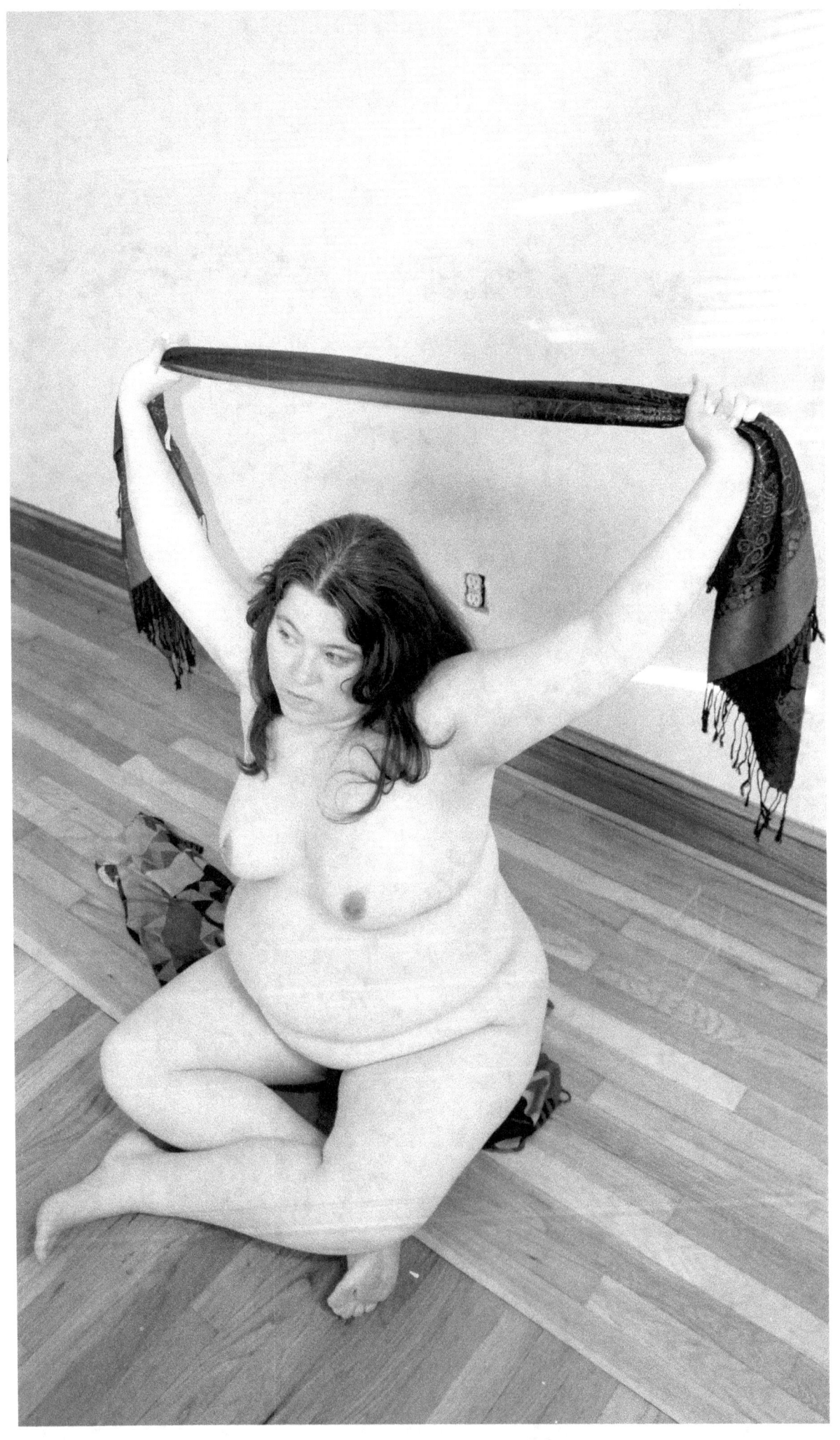

6

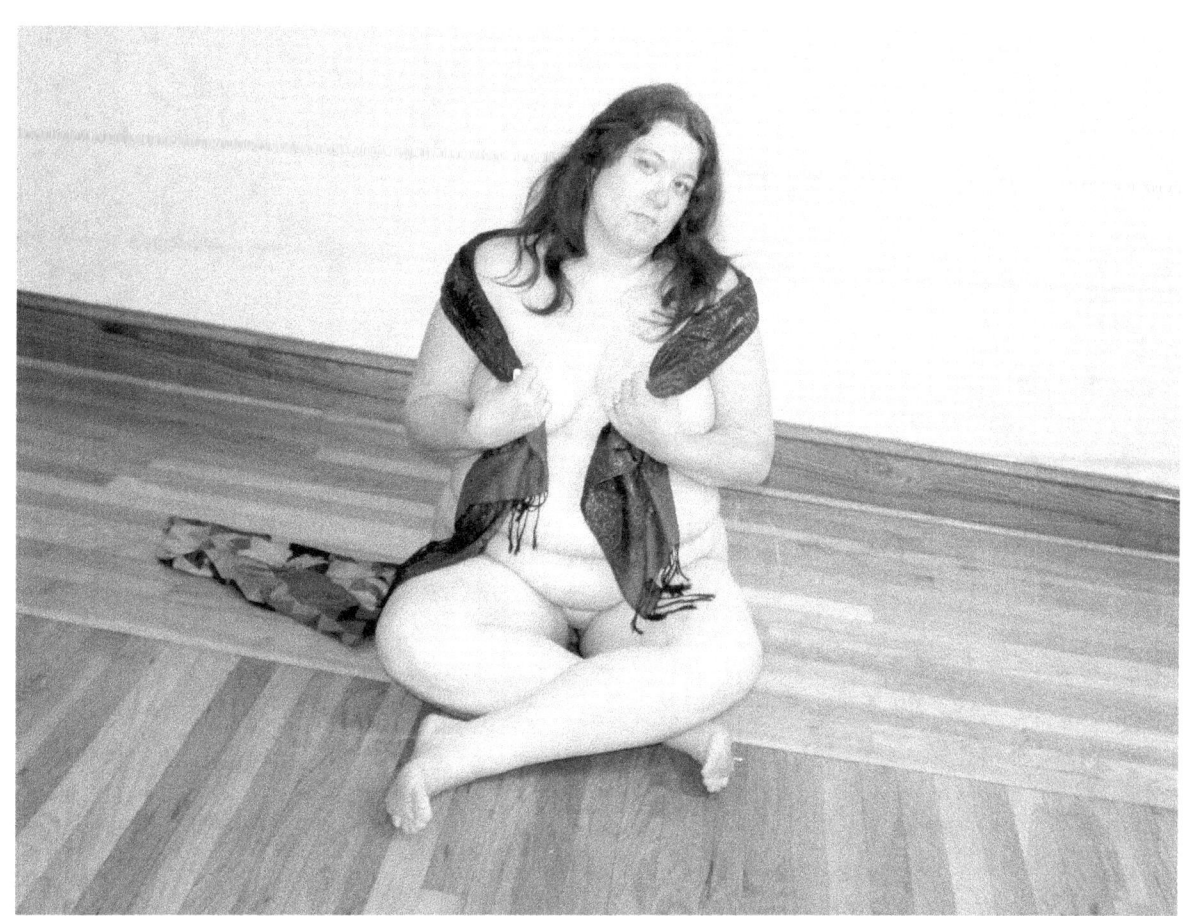

7

8

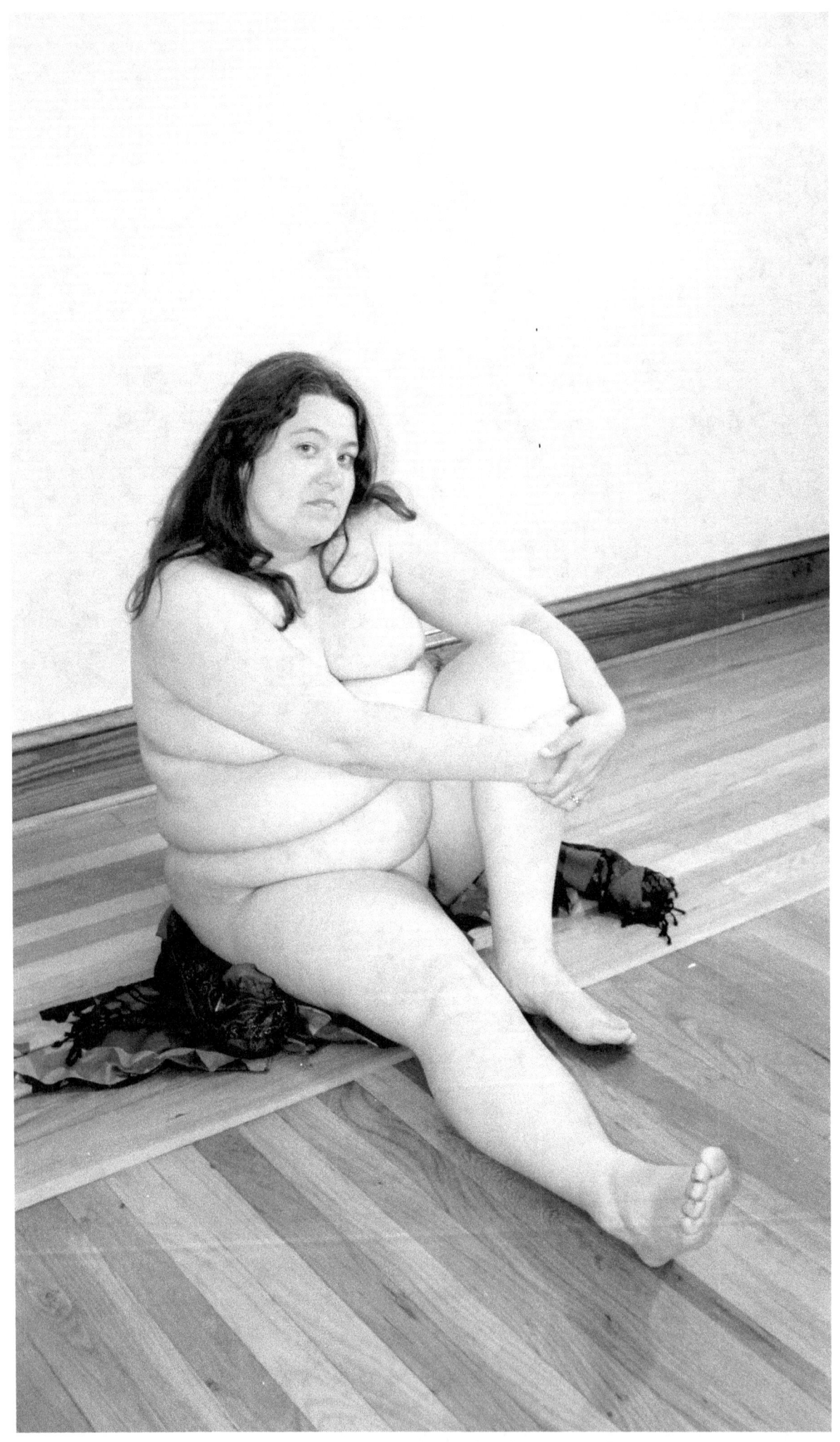

9

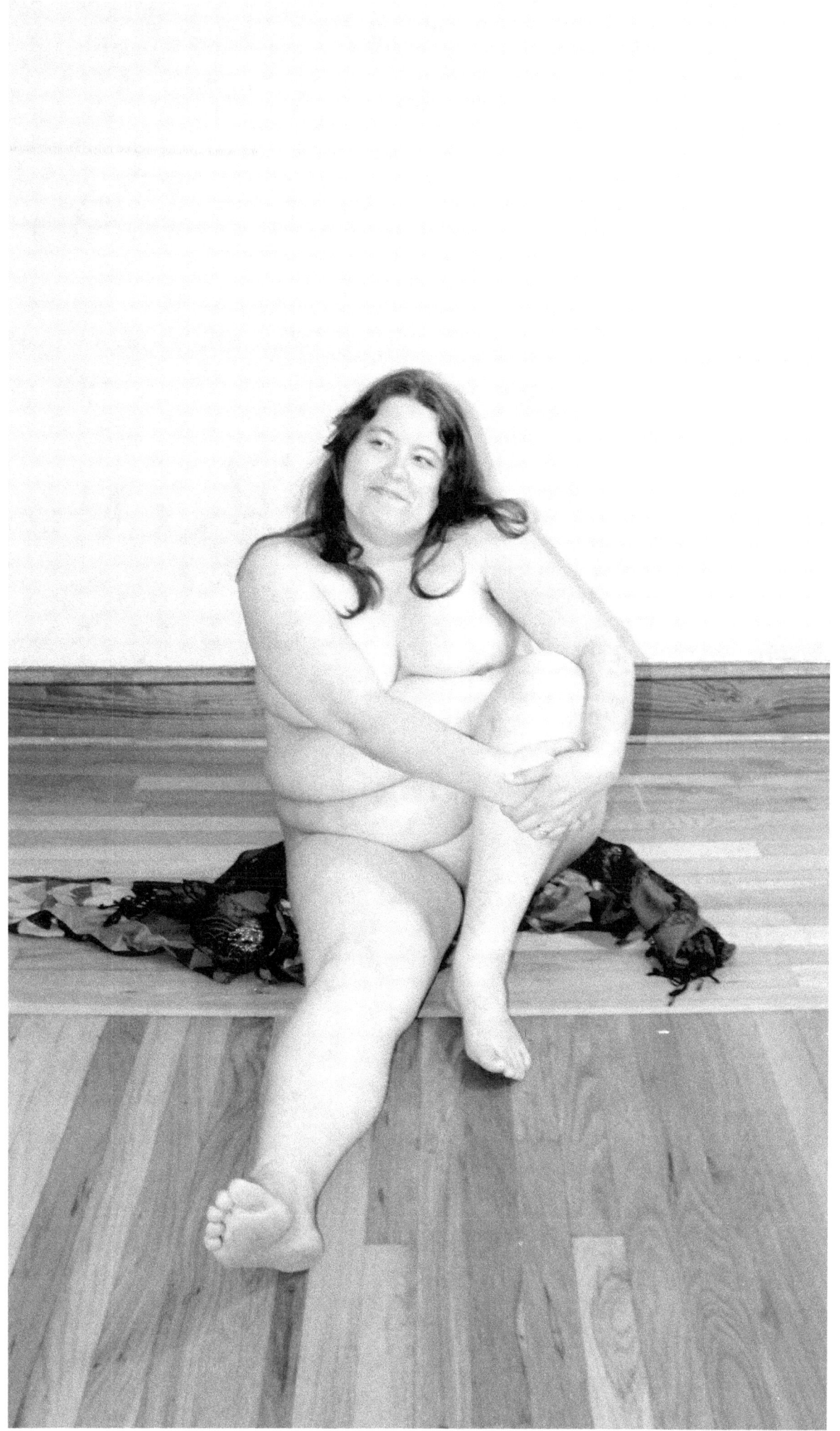

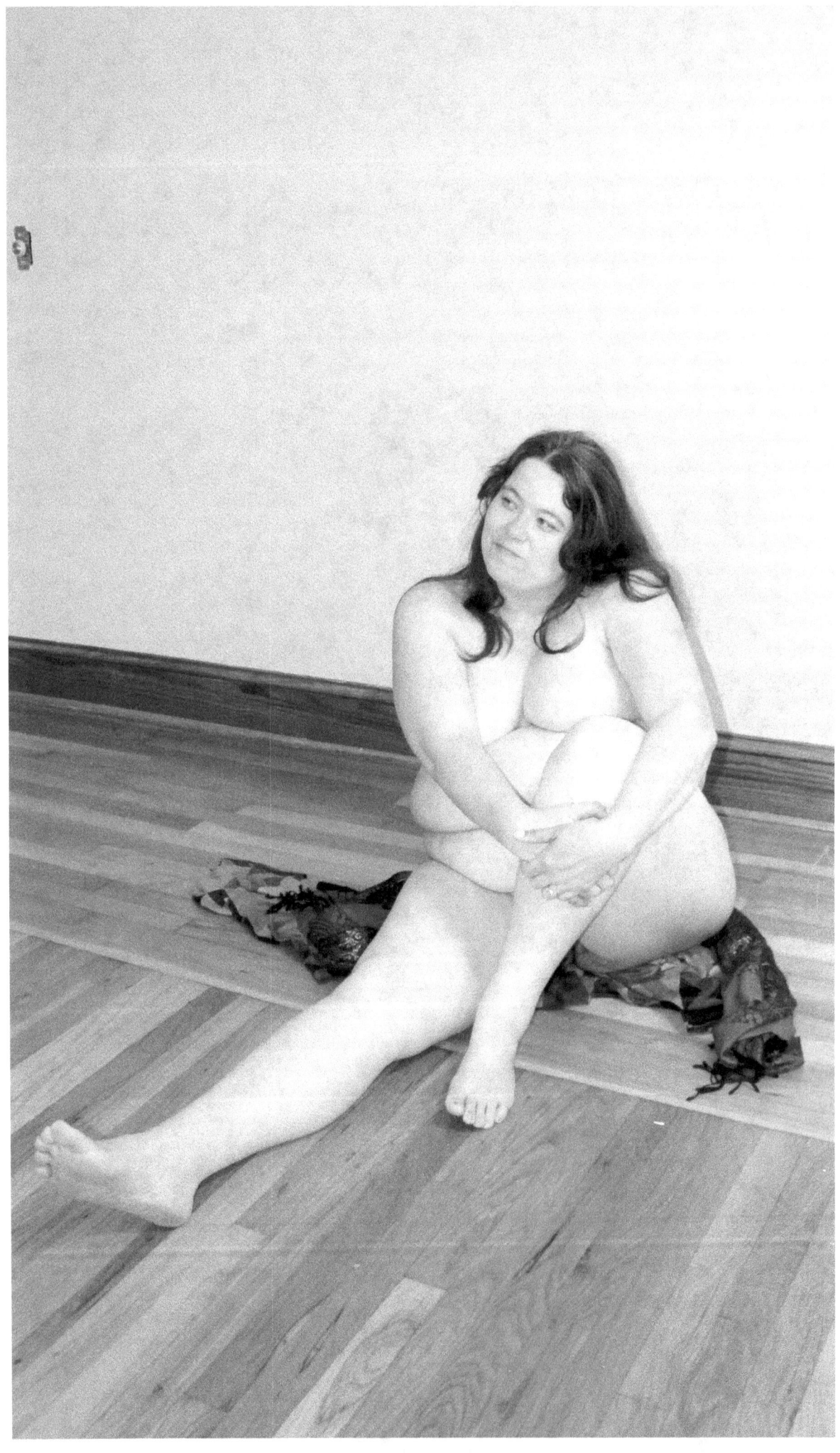

11

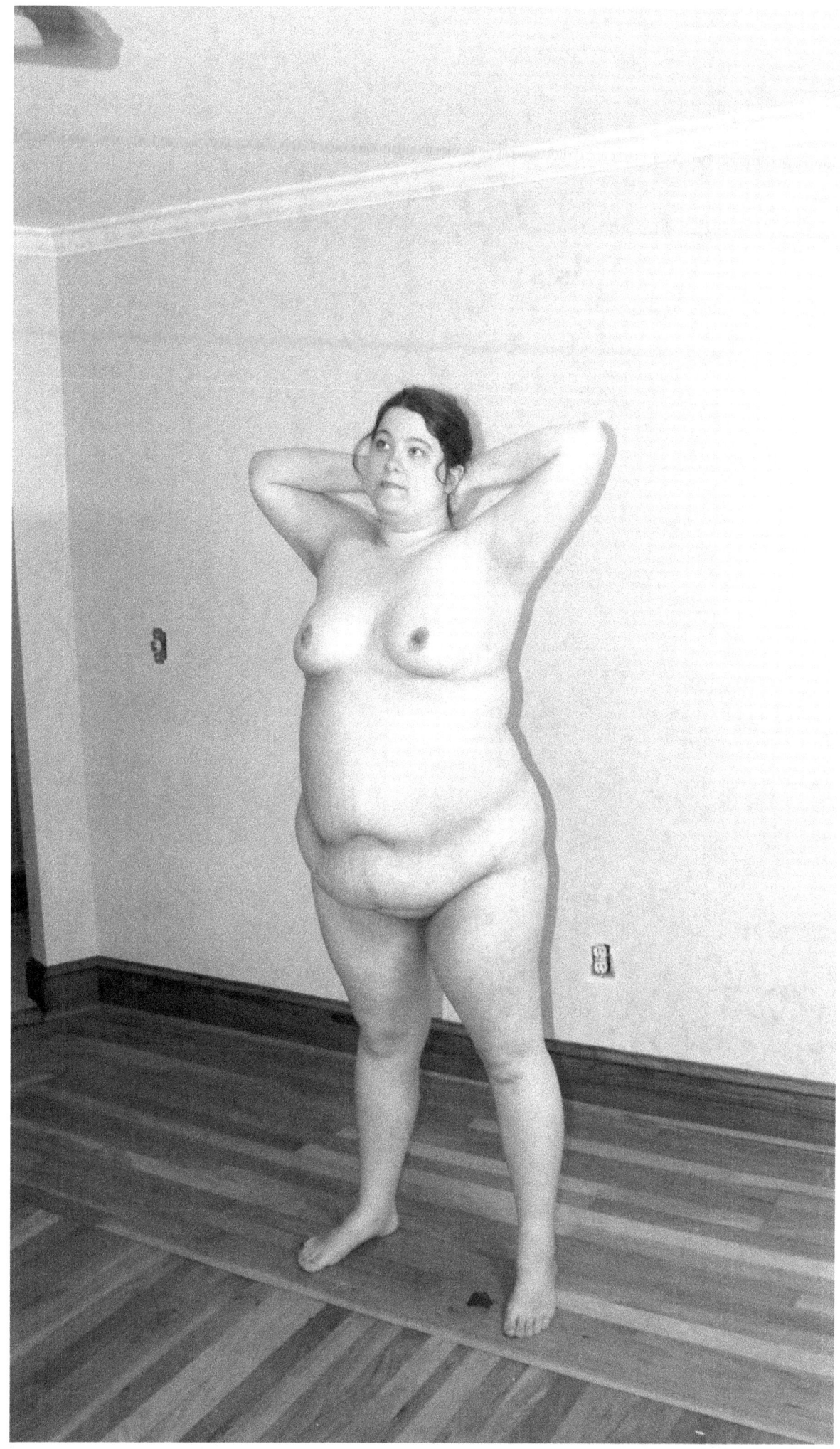

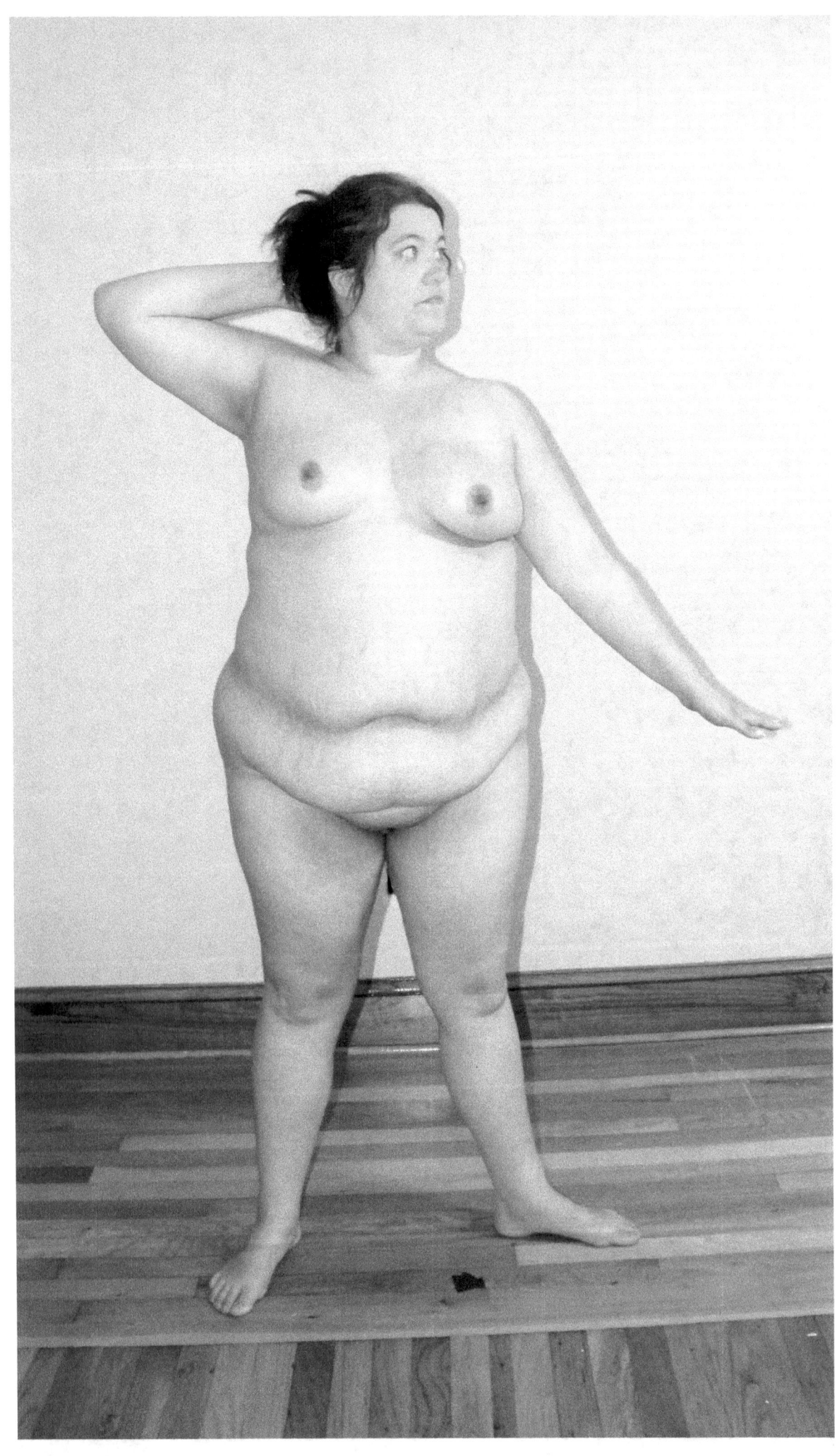

13

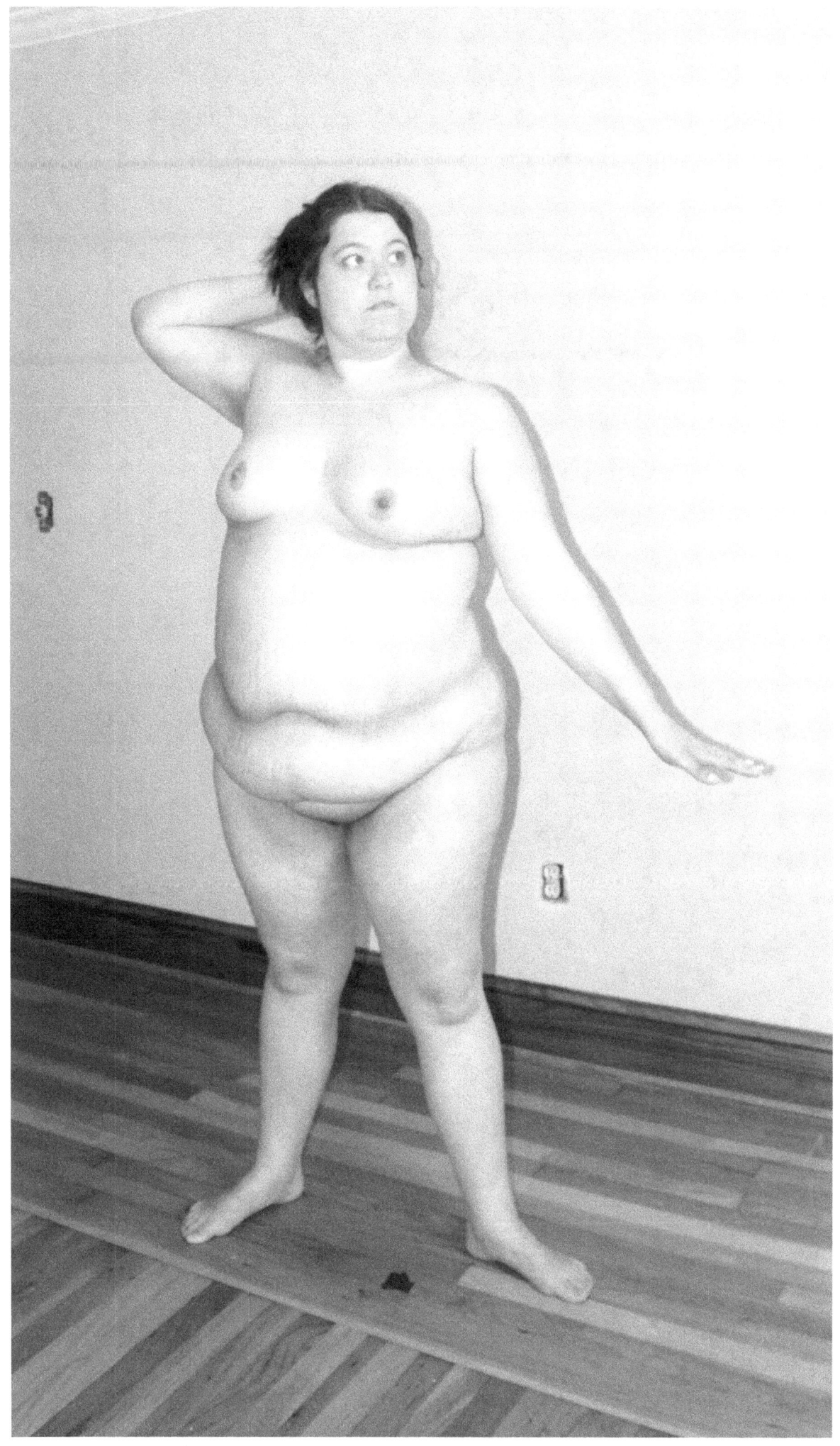

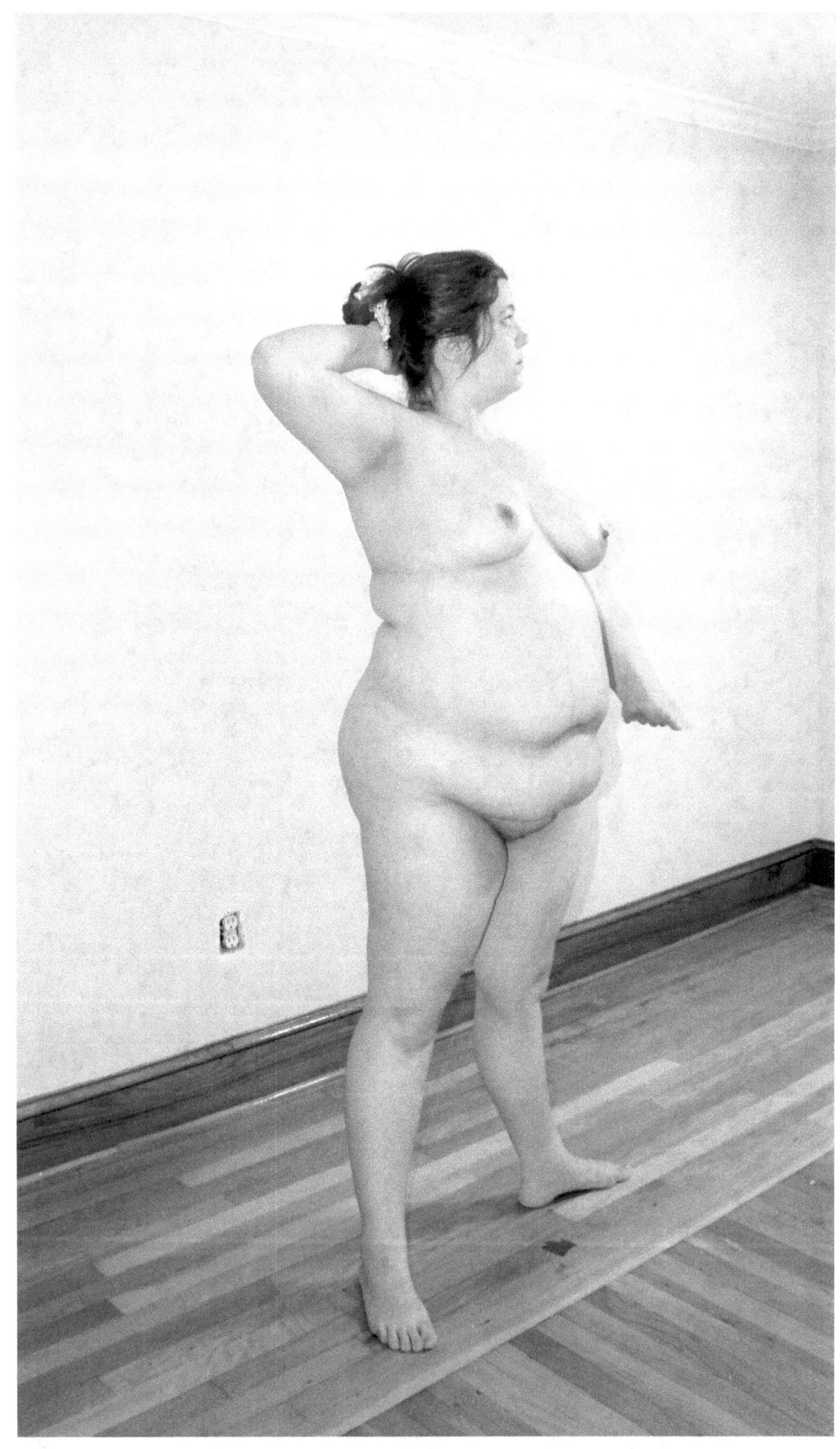

15

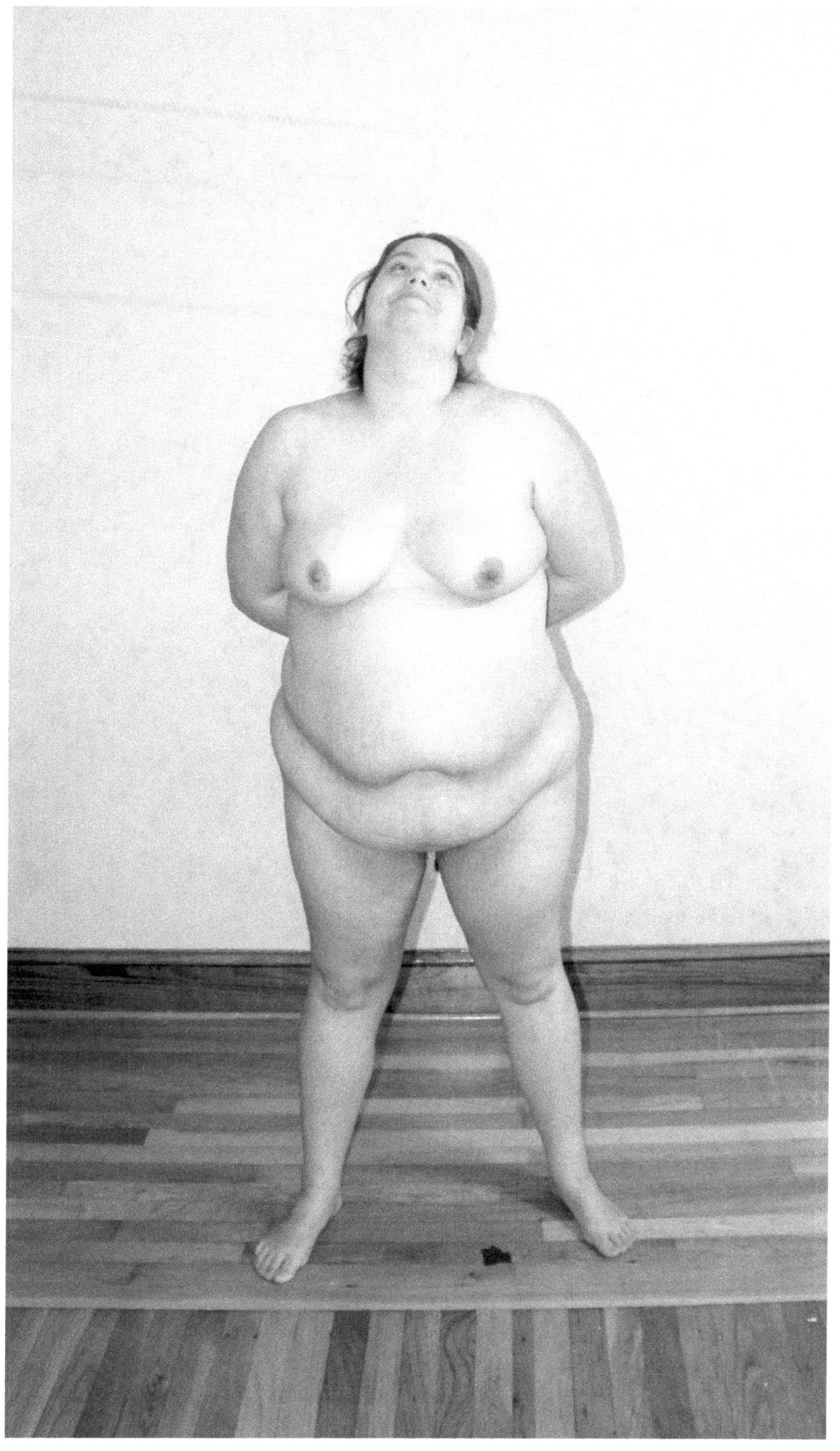

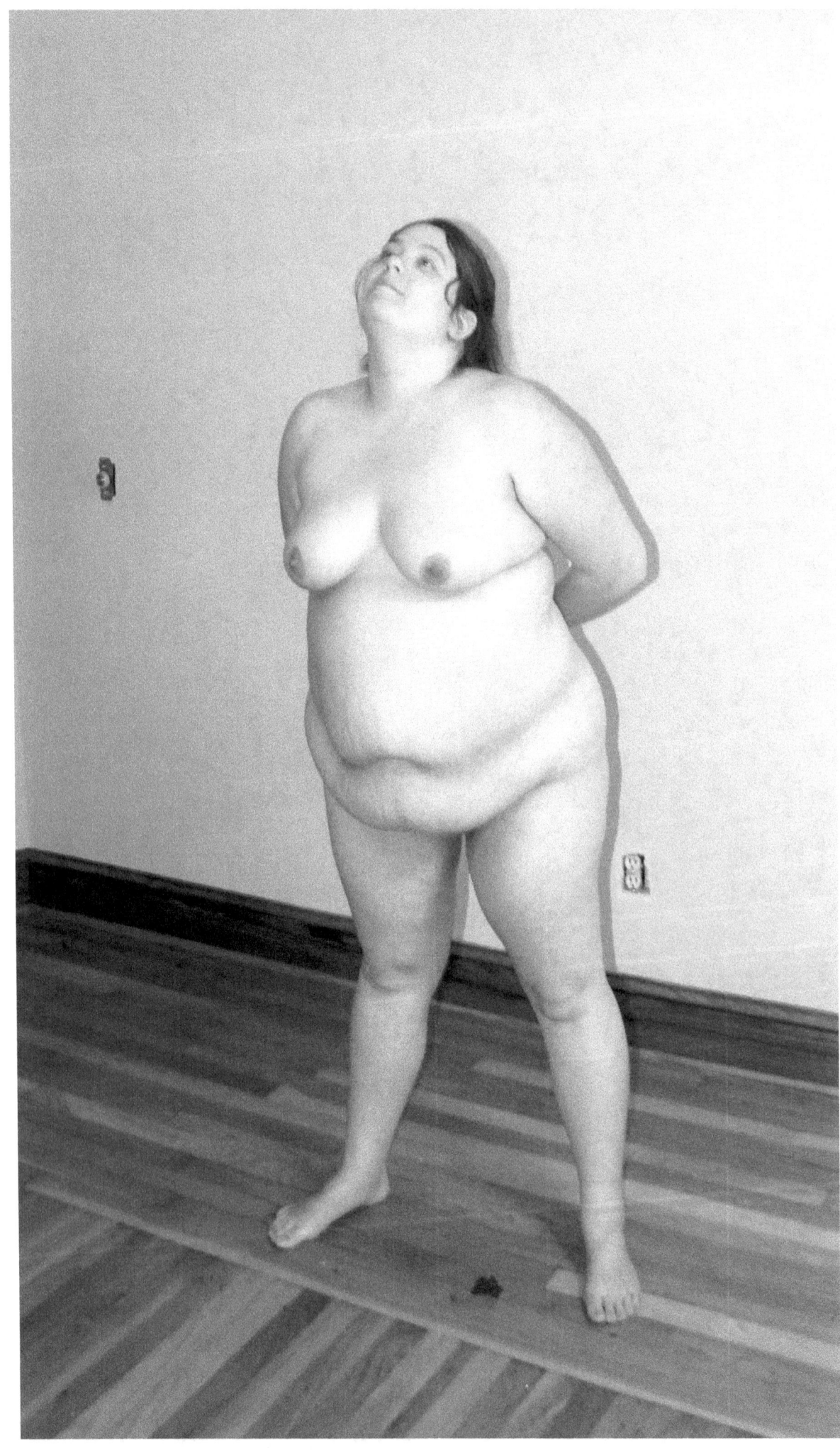

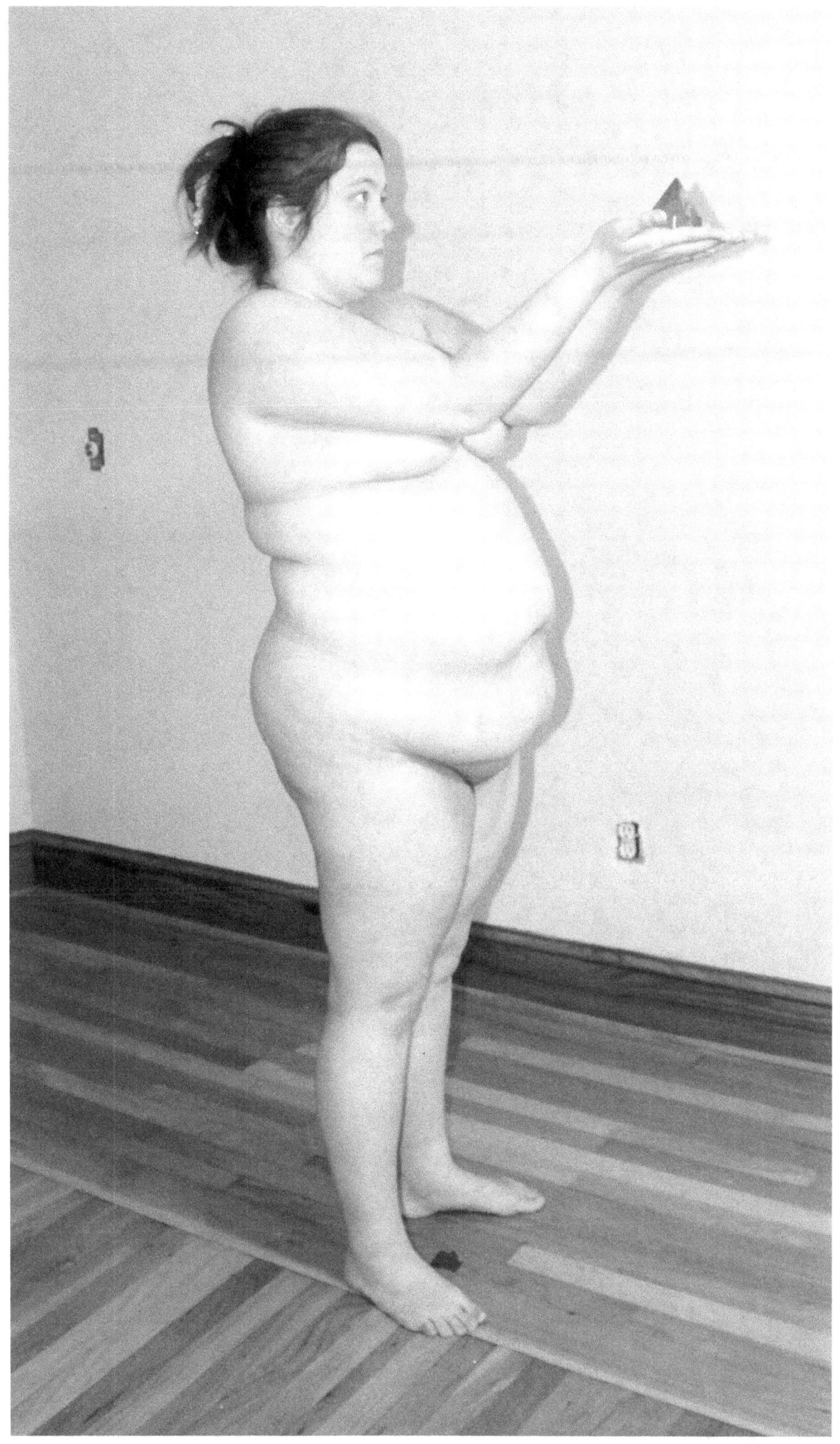

18

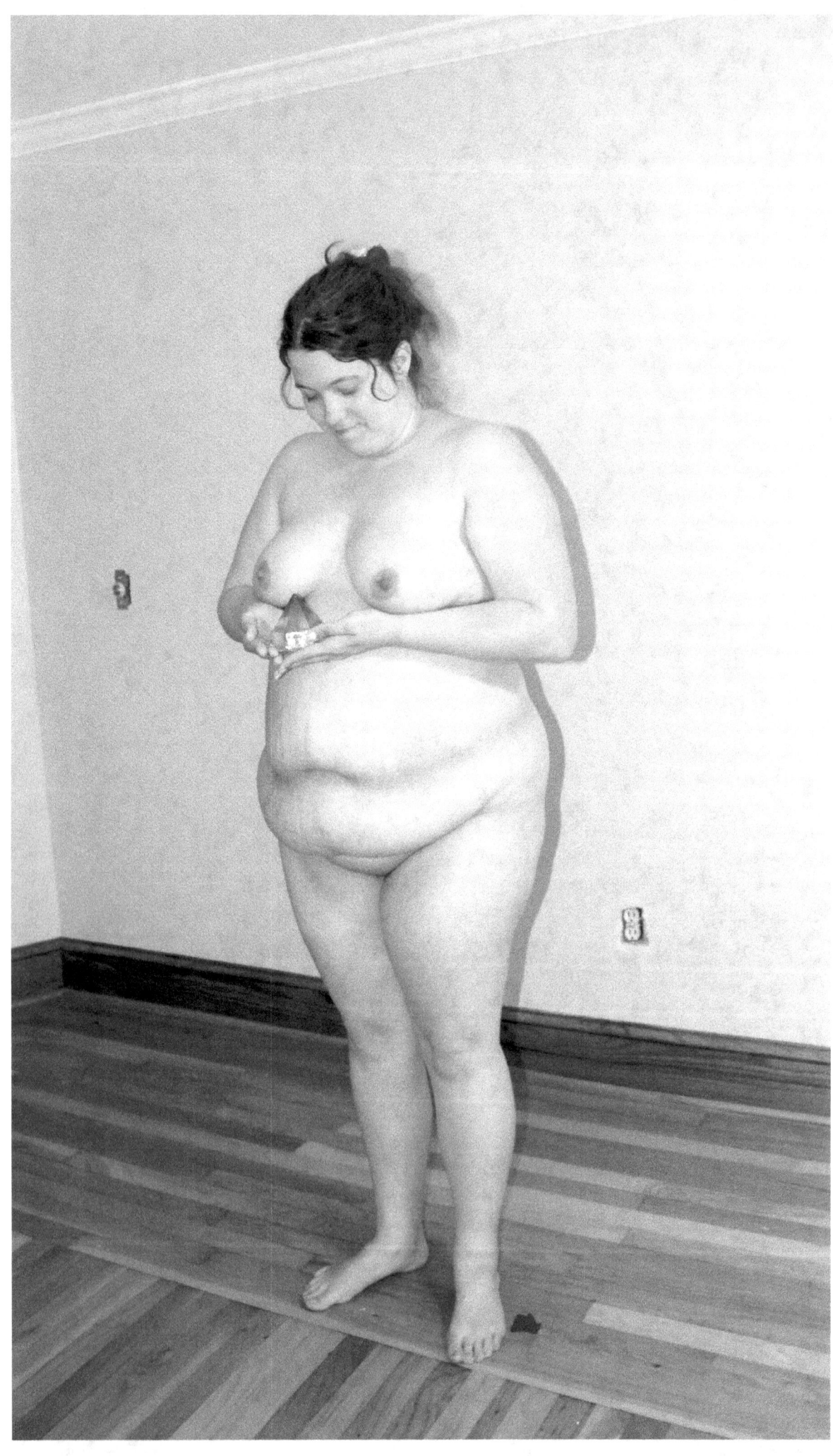

19

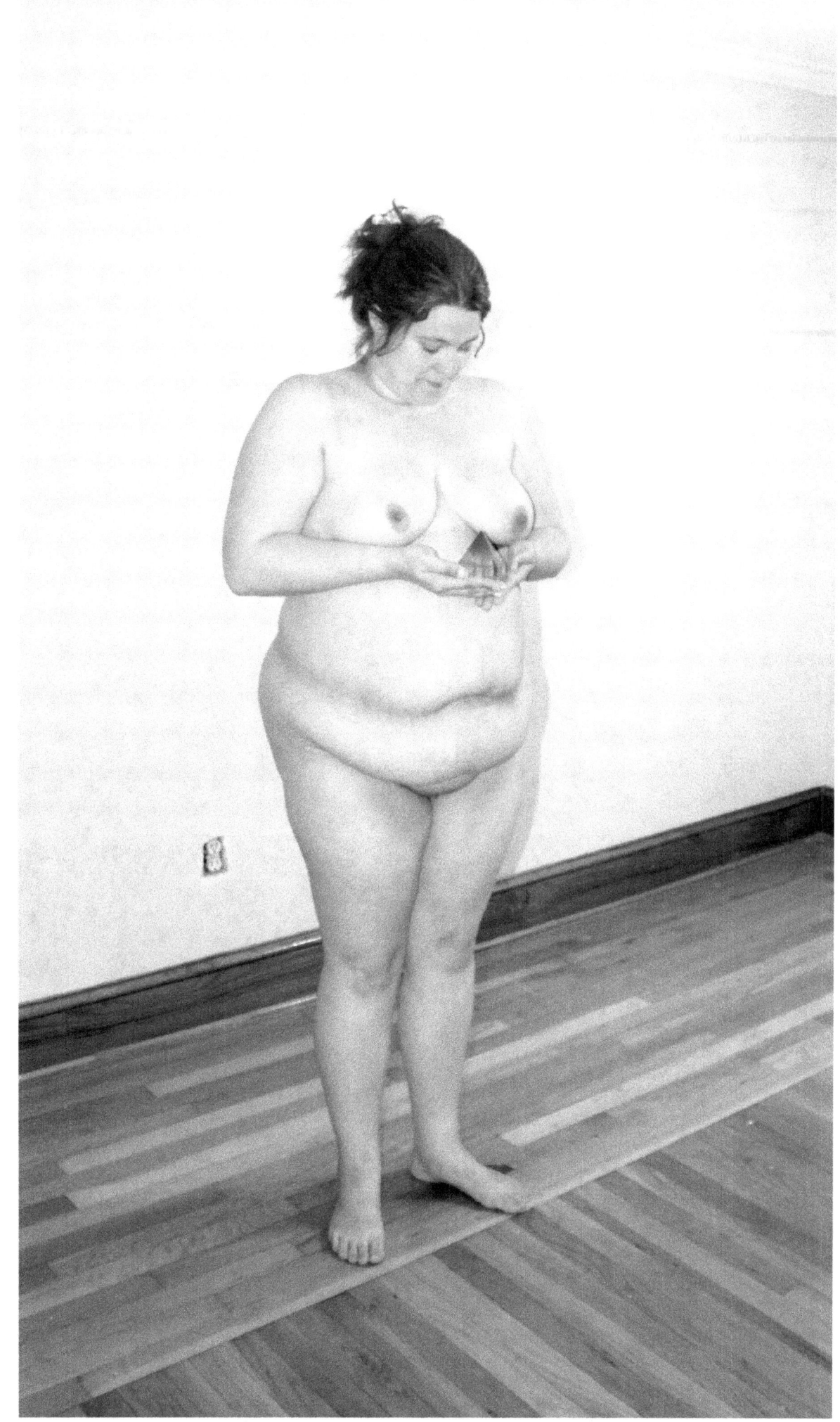

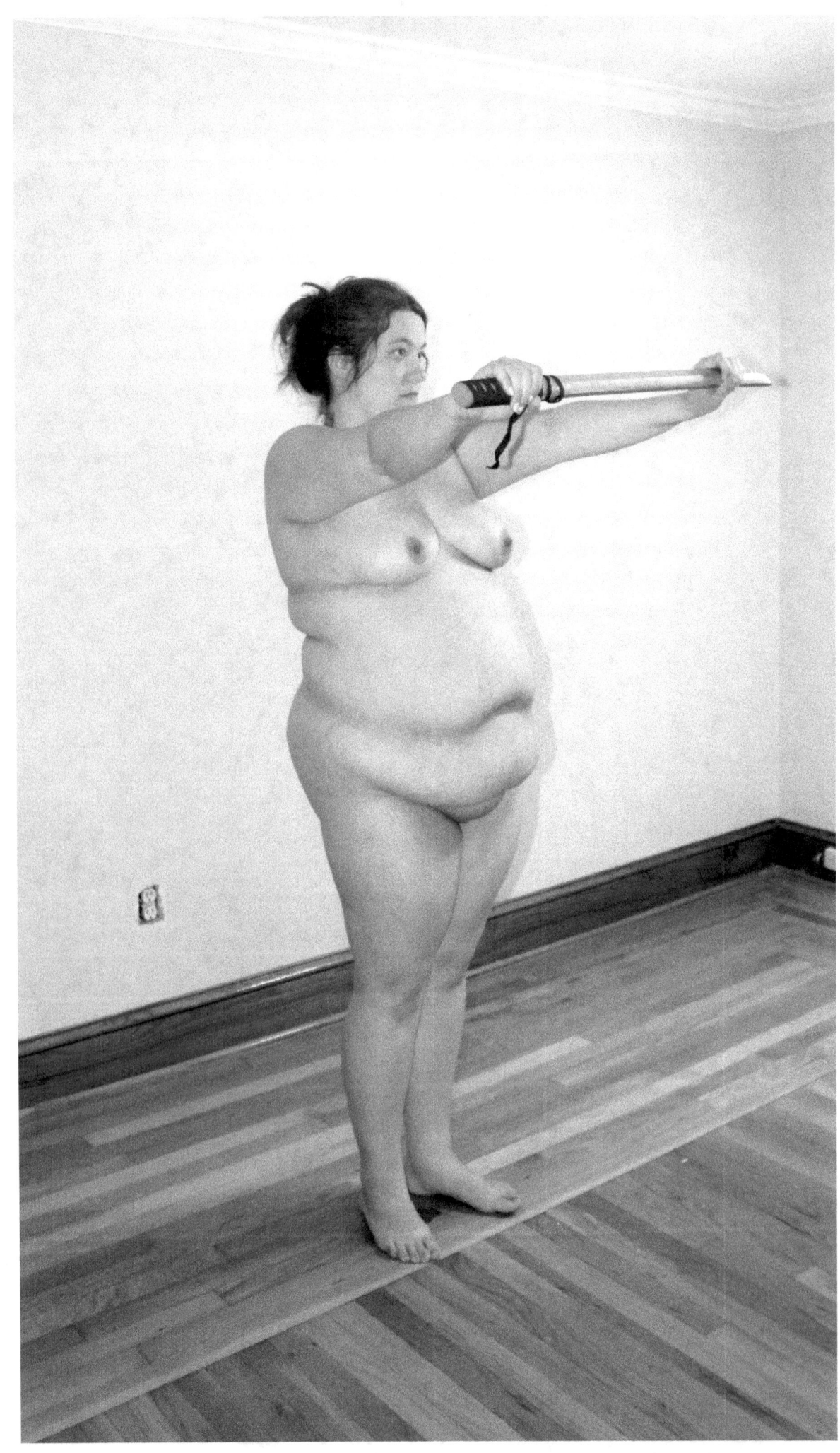

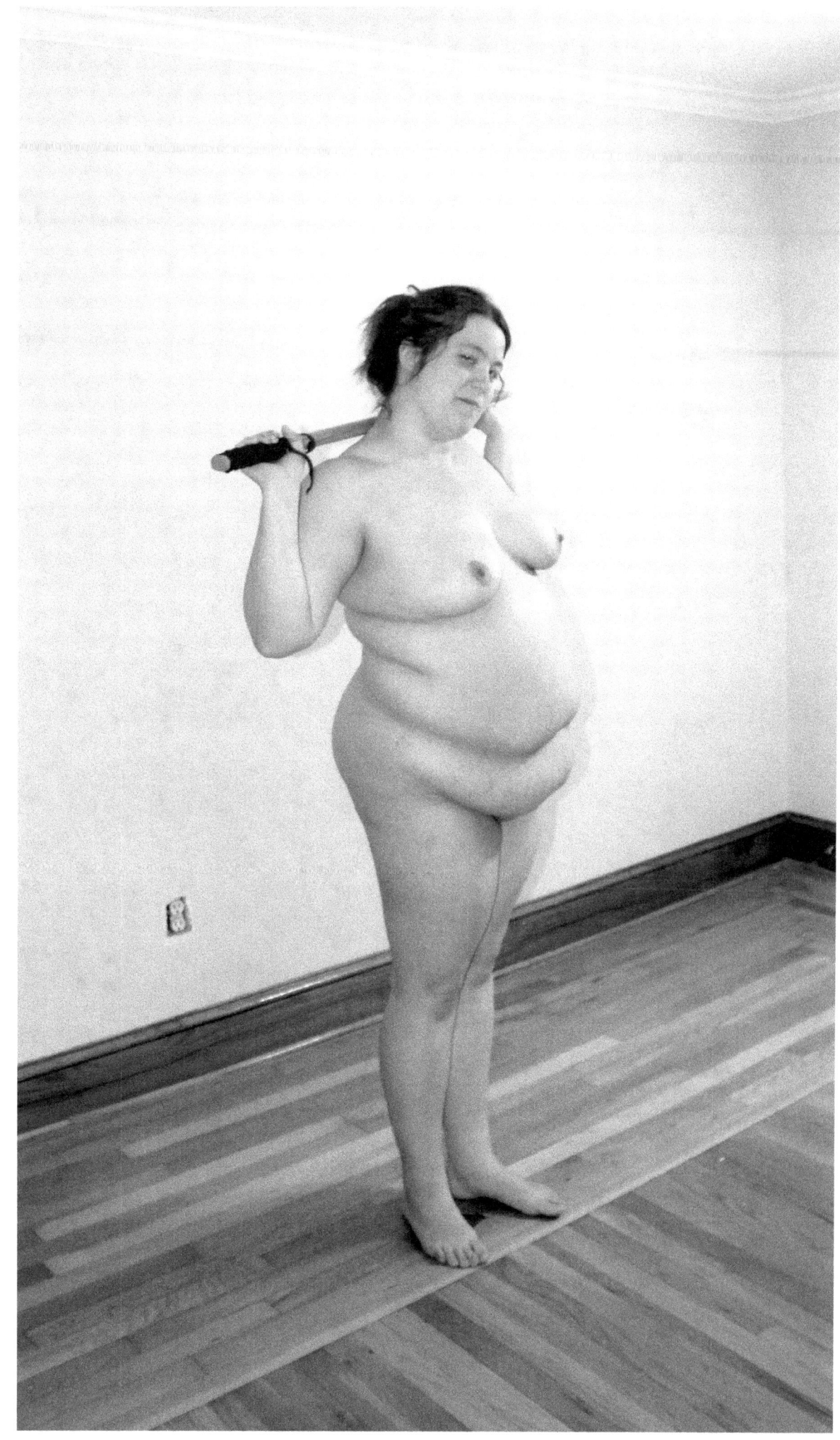

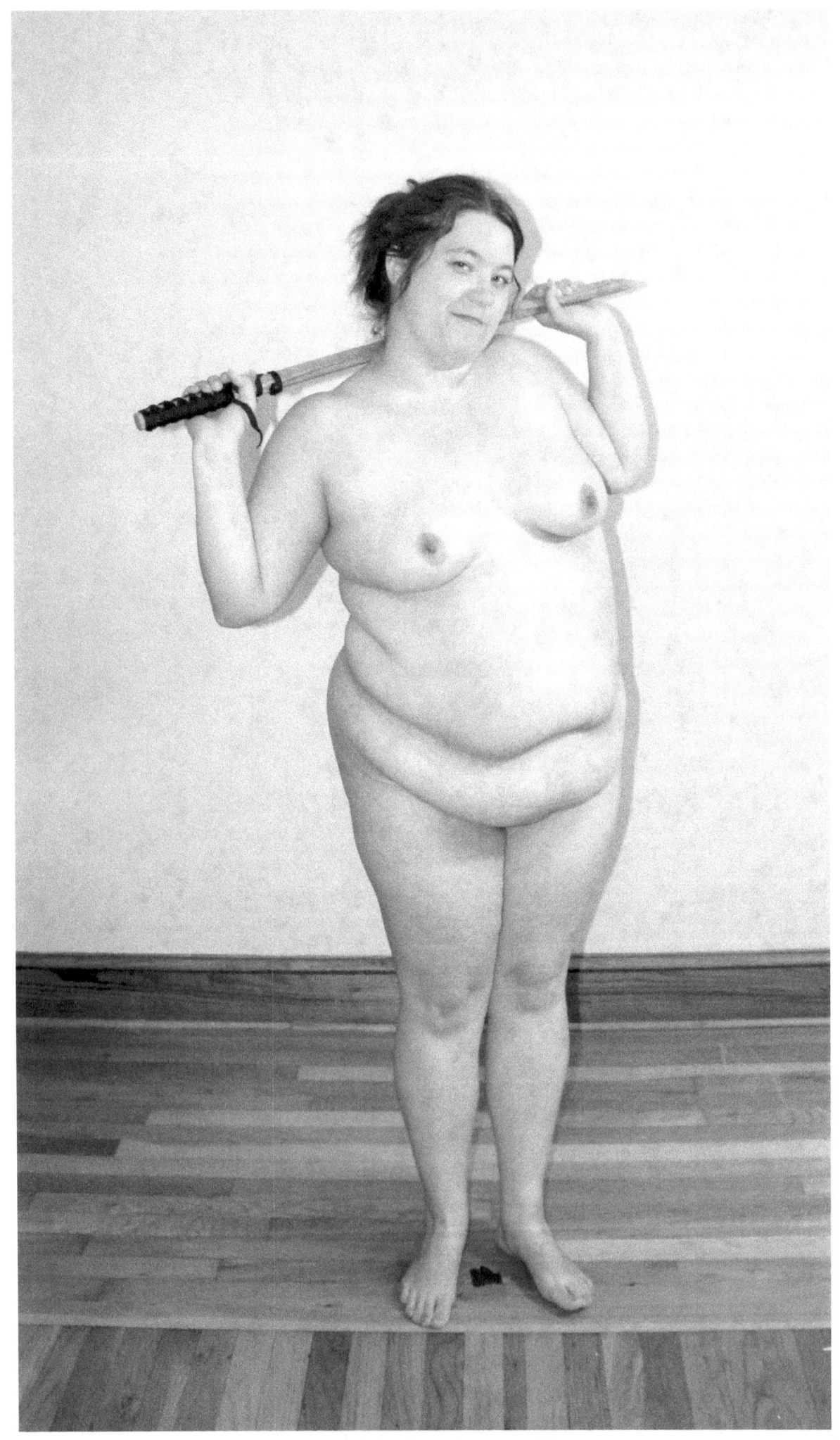

23

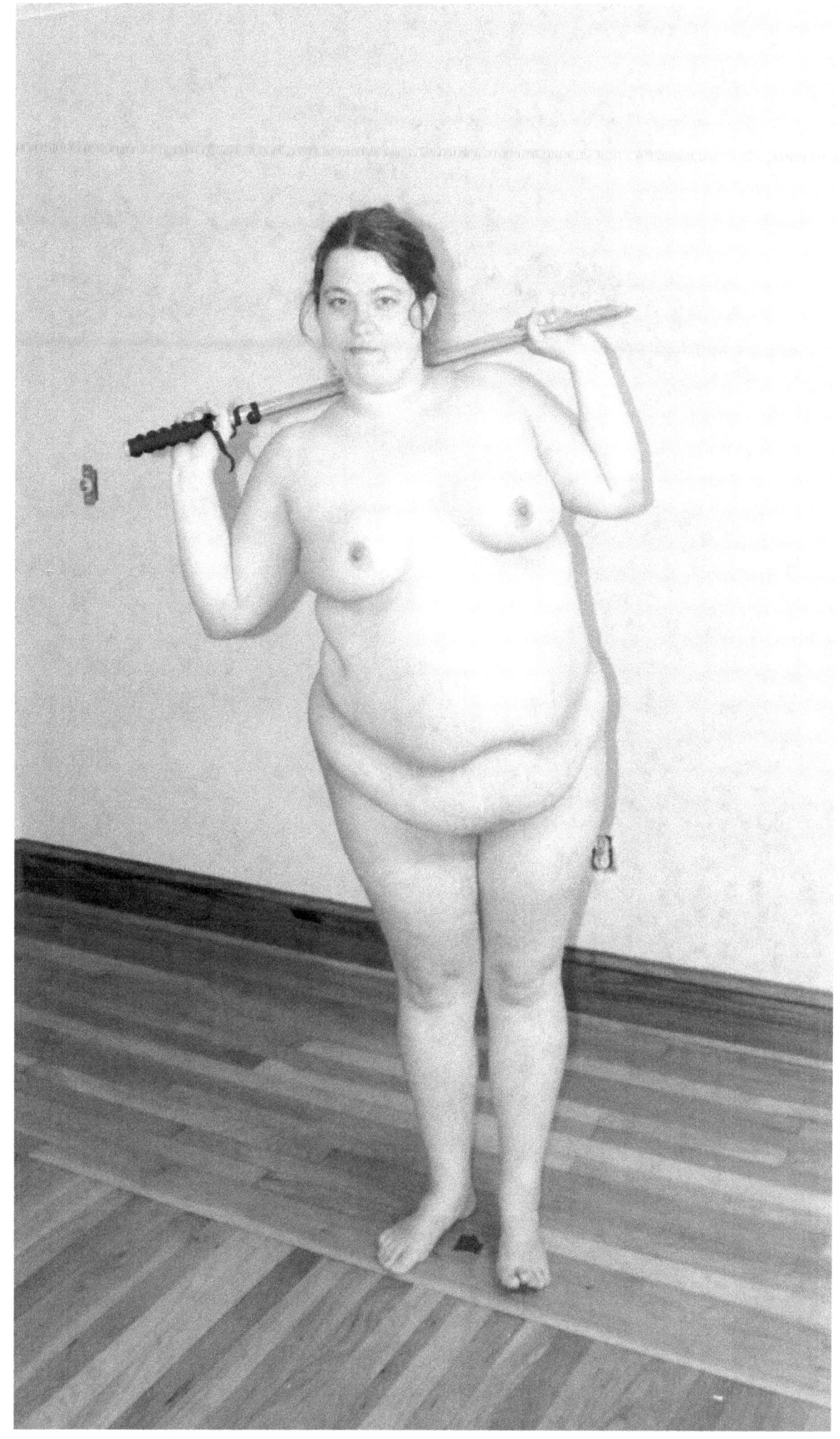

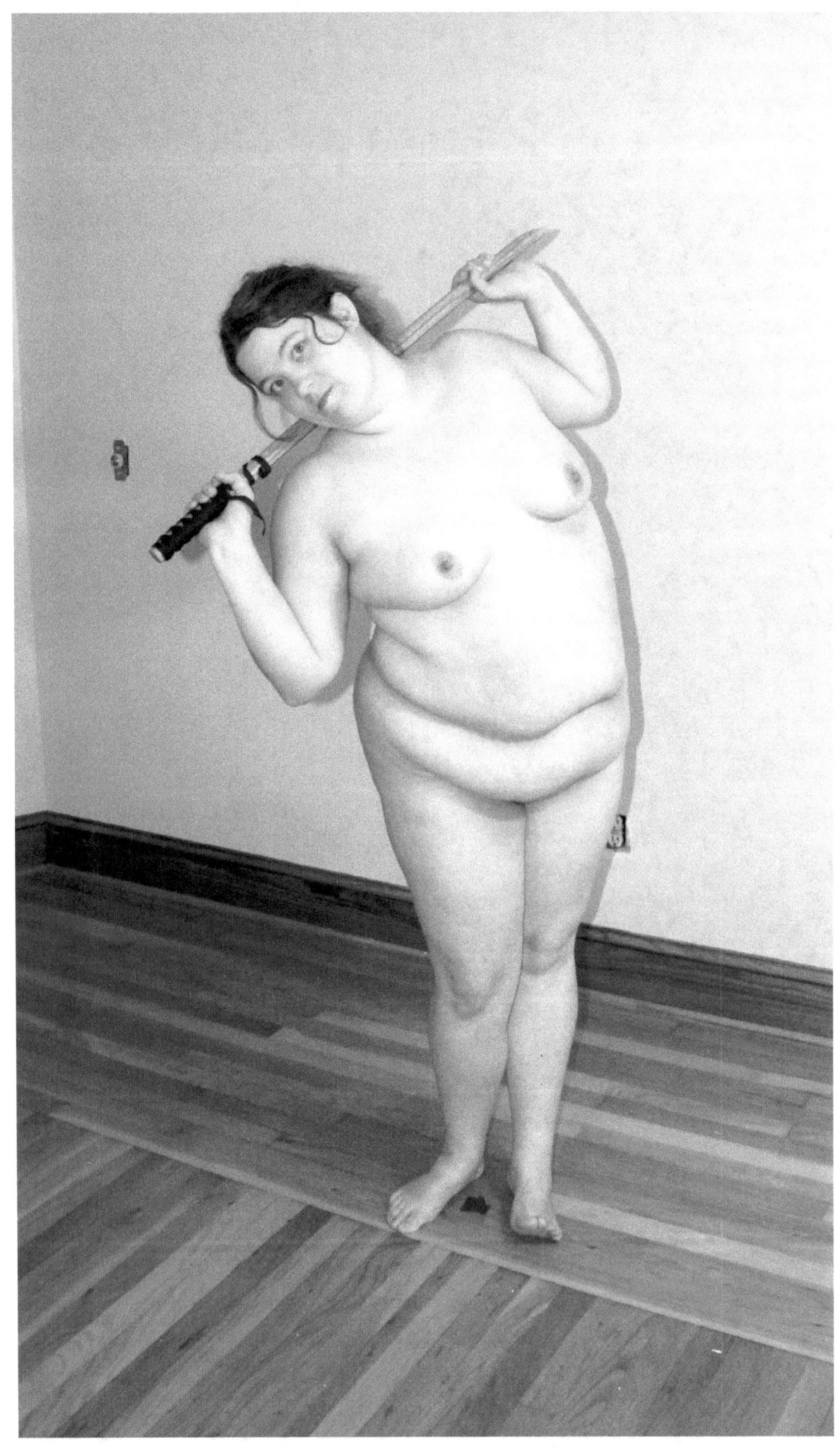

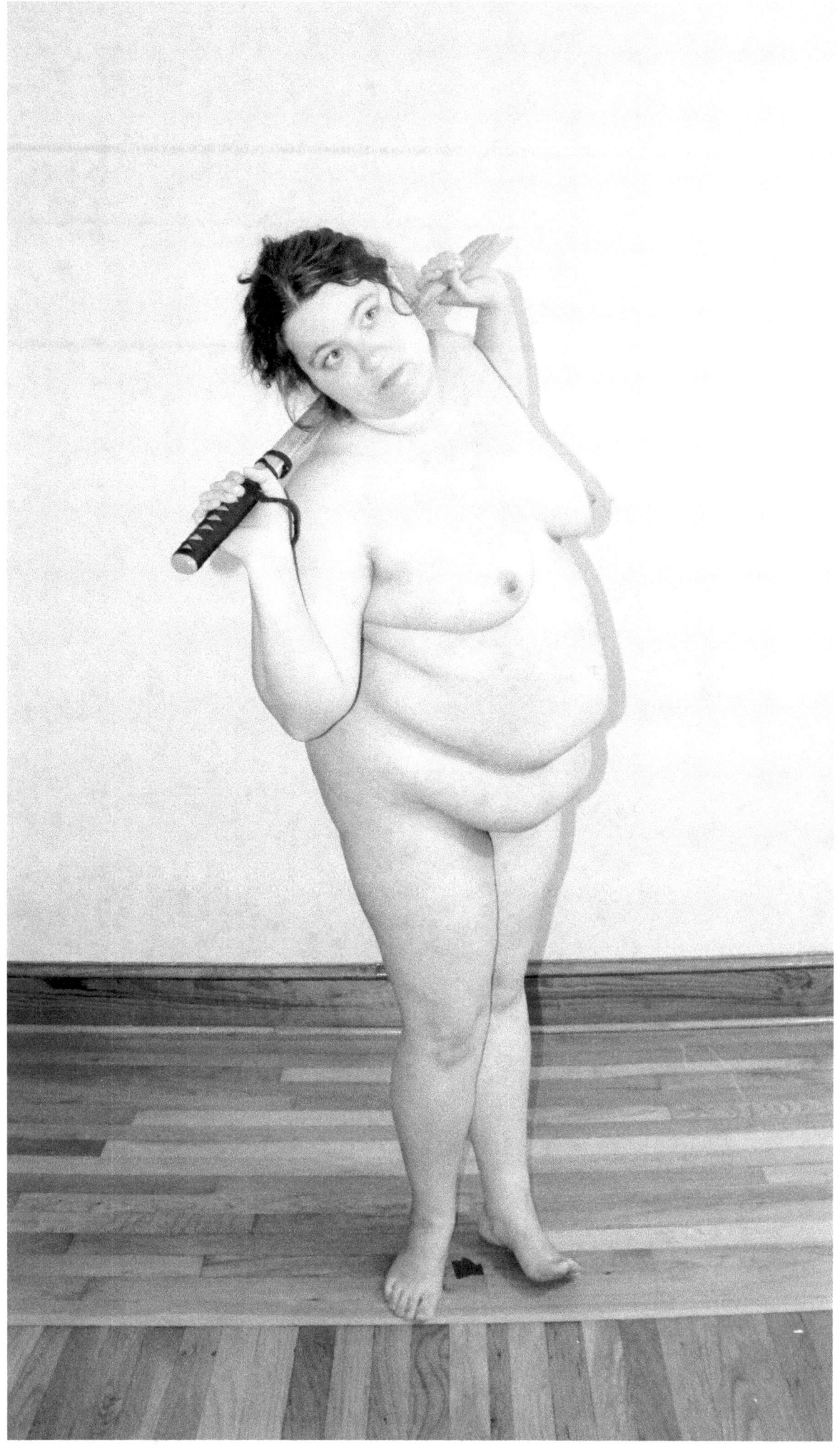

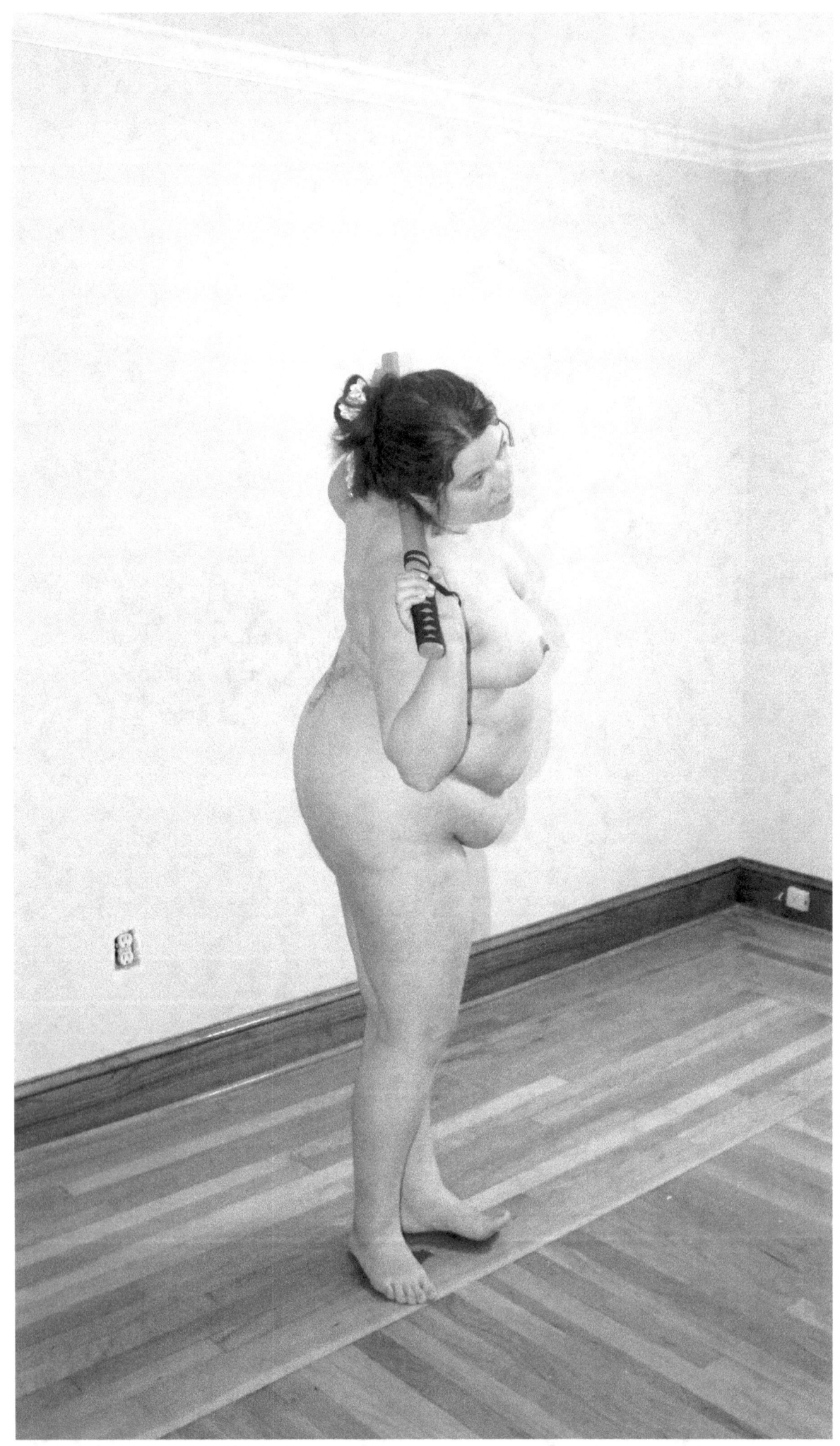

27

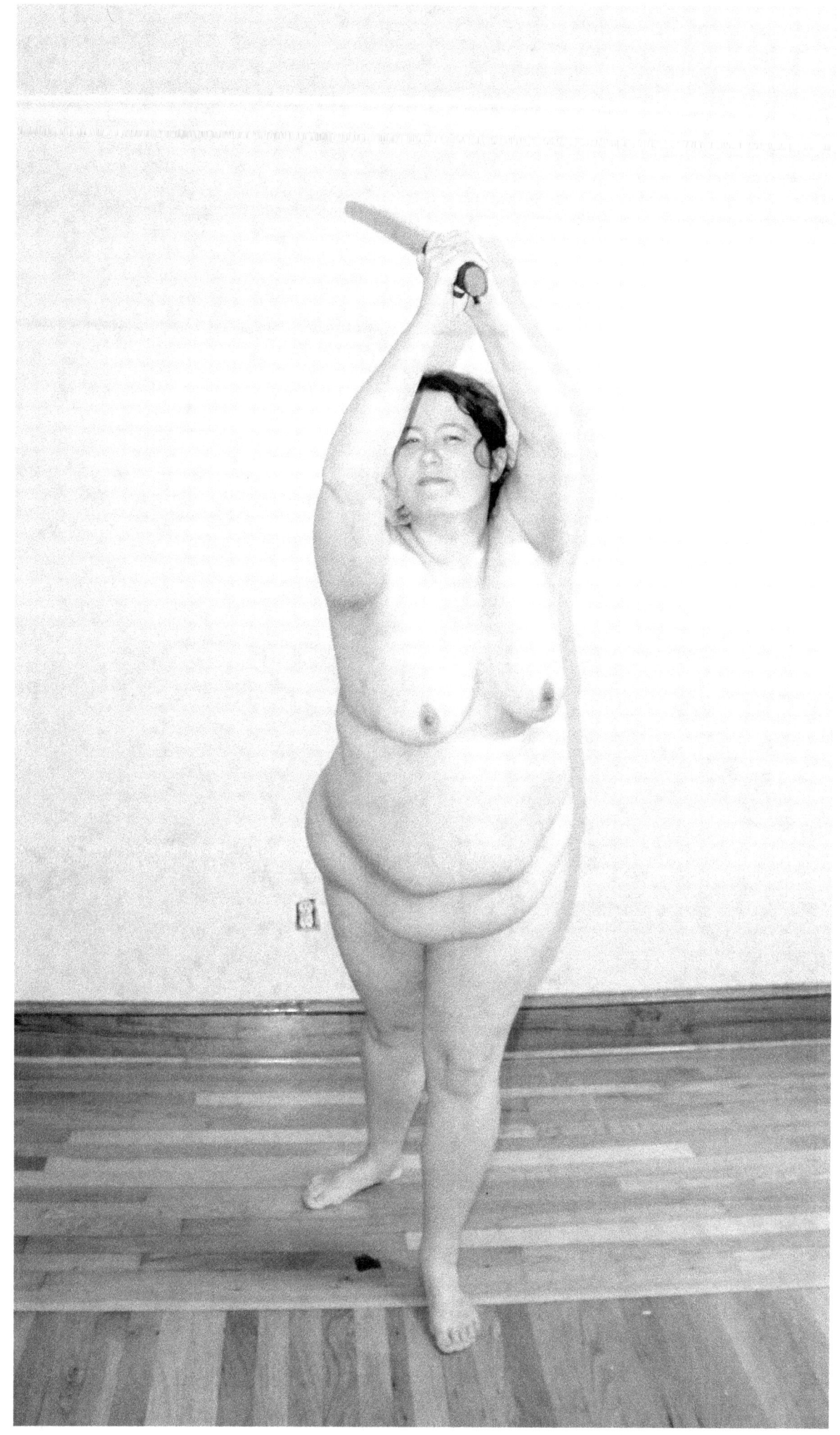

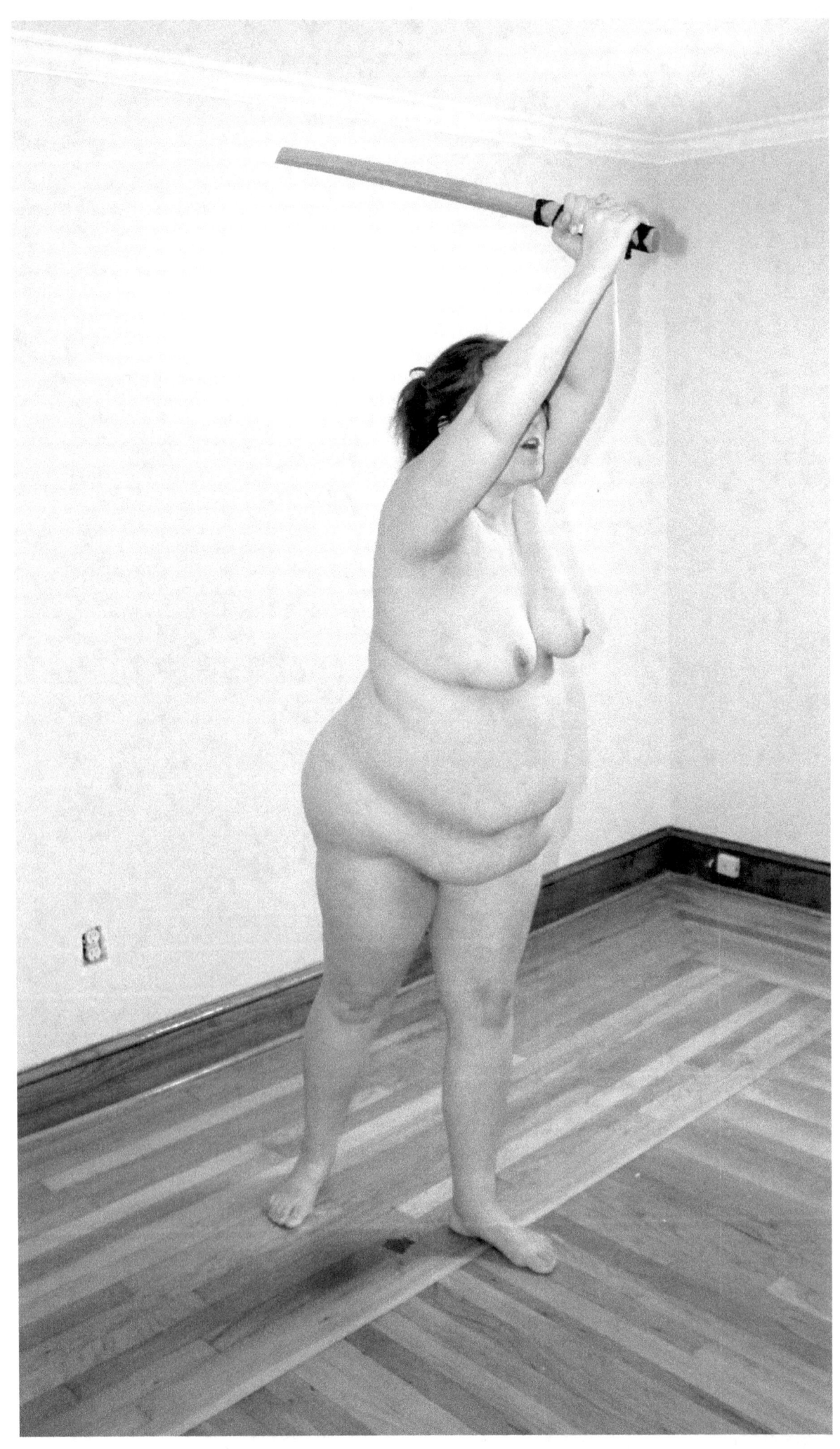

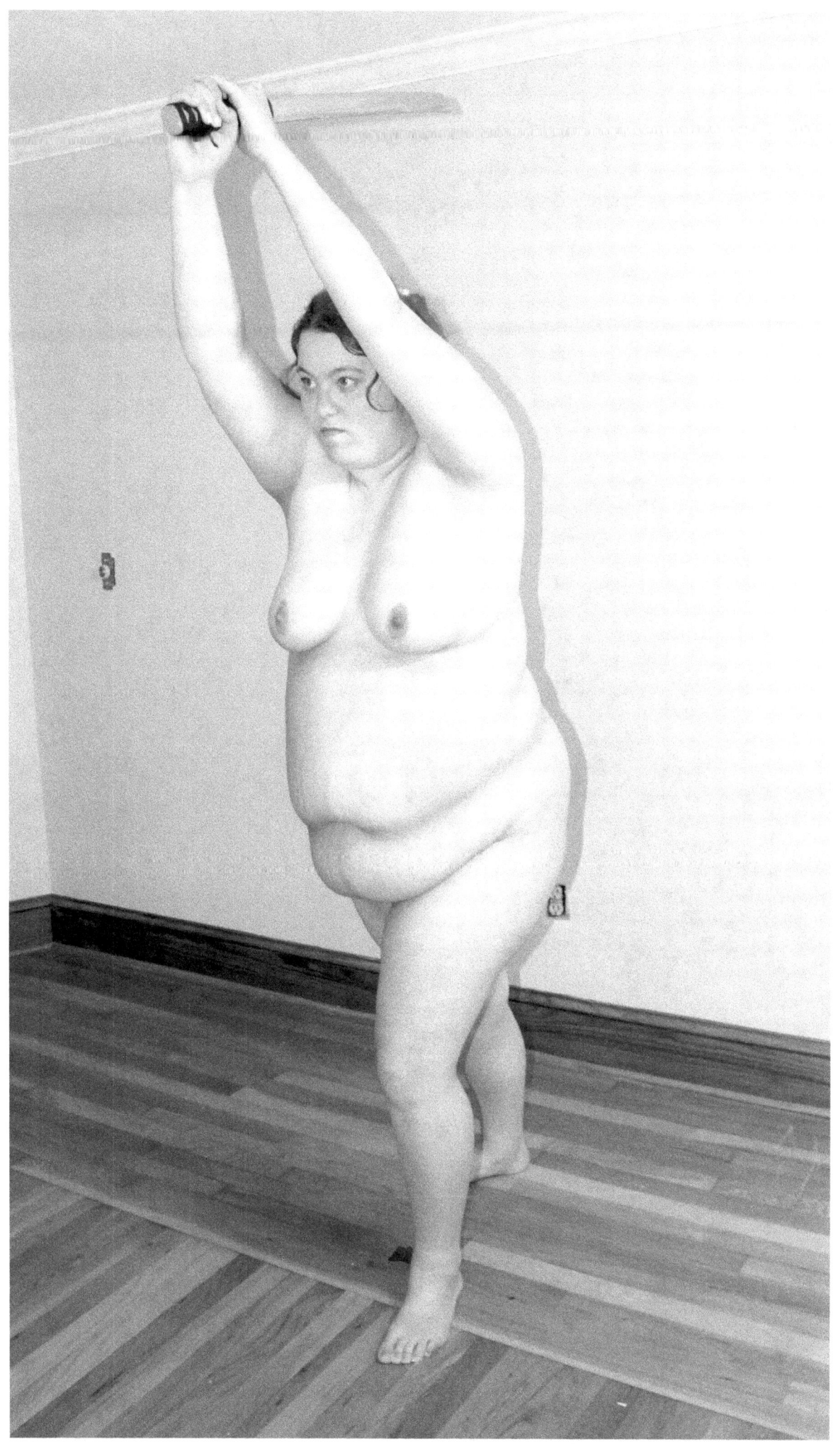

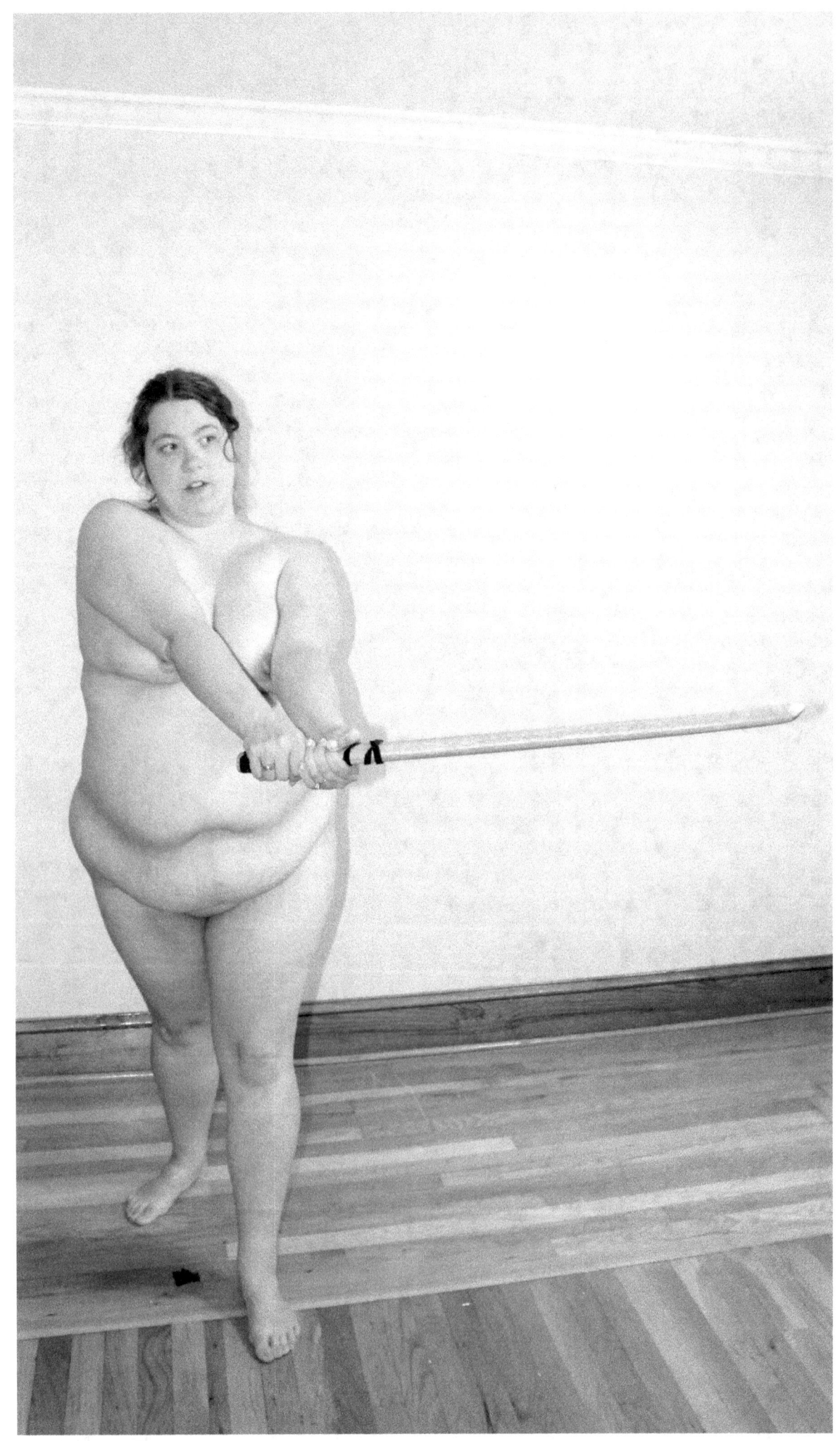

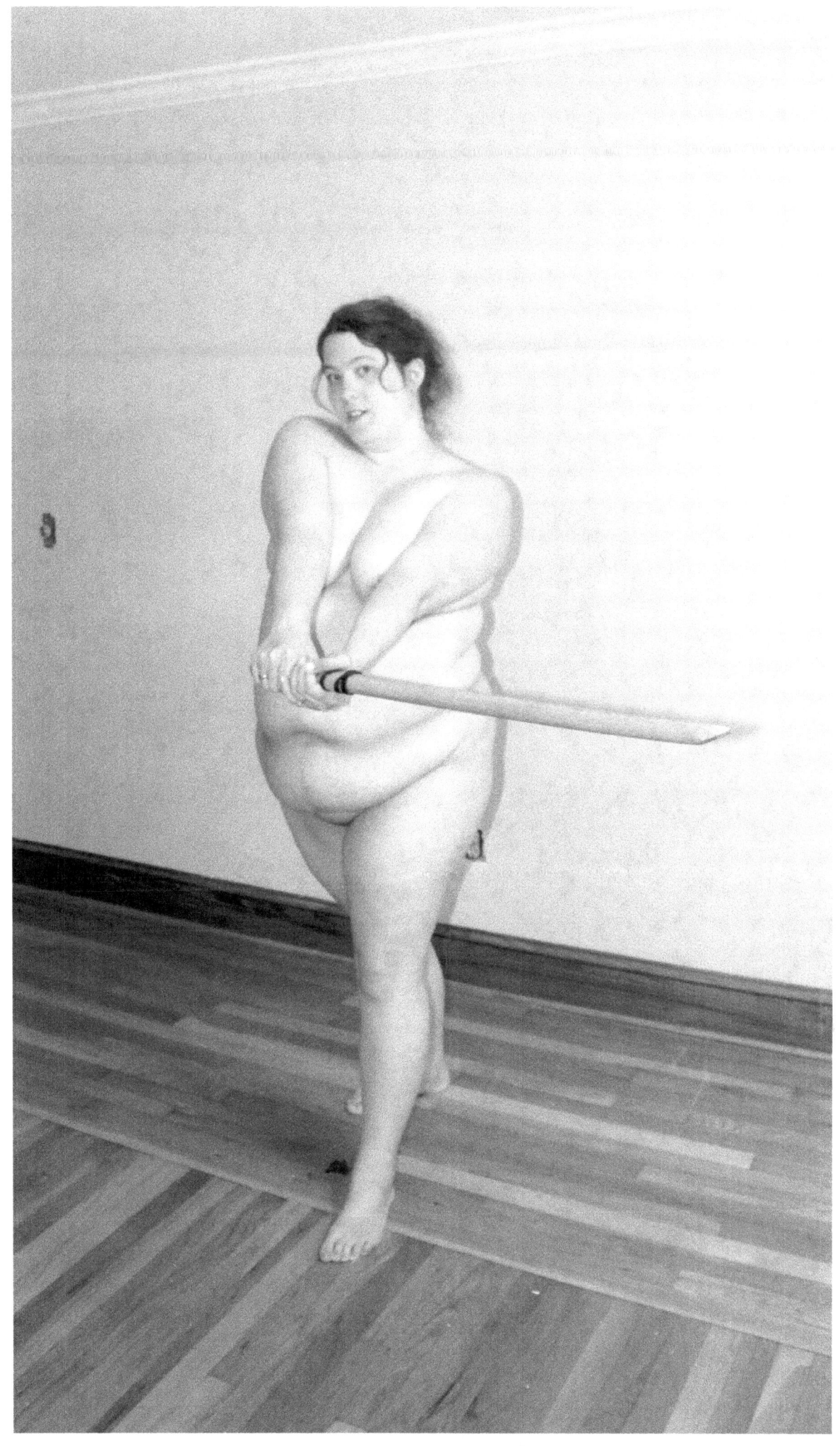

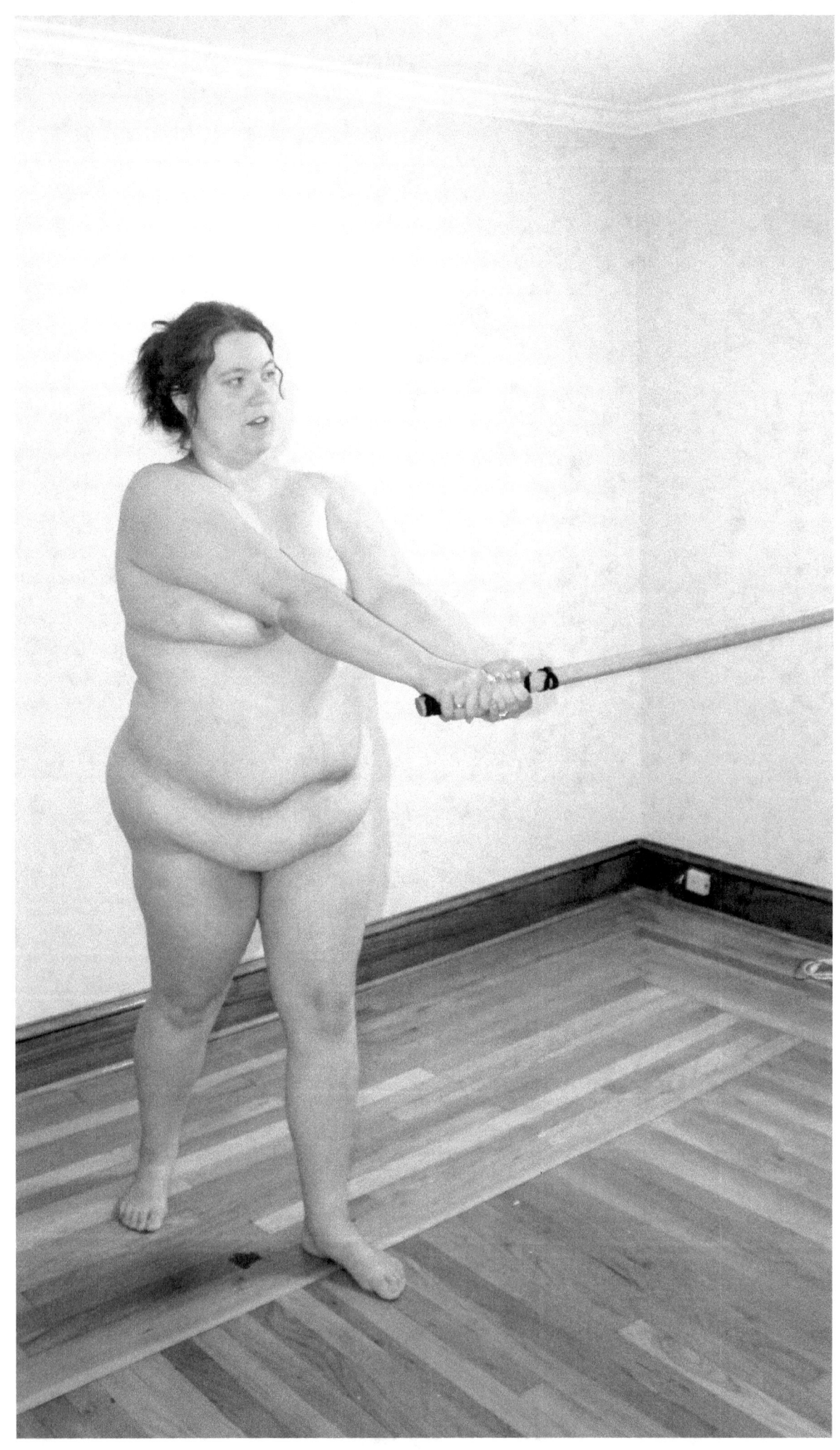

33

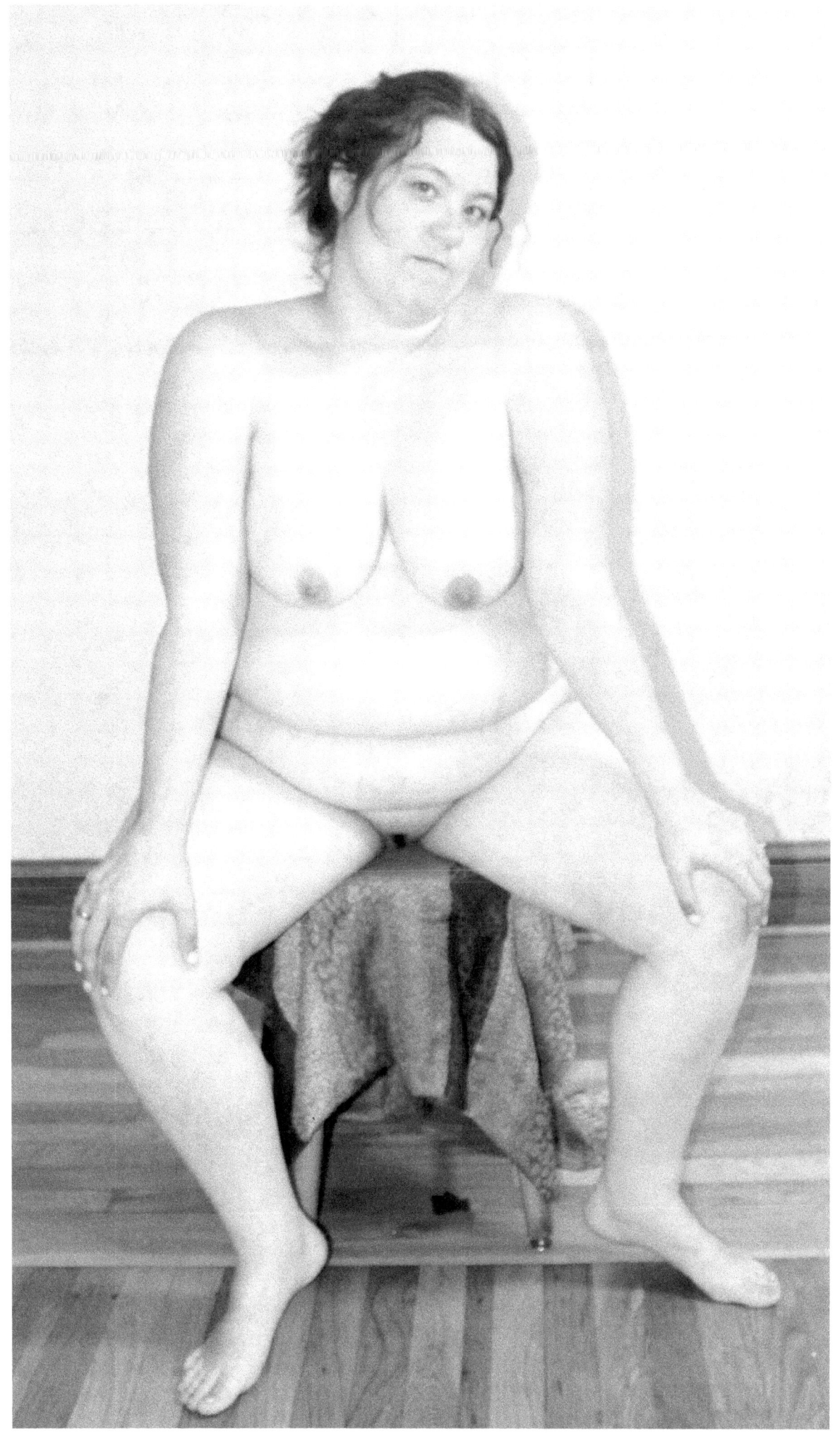

34

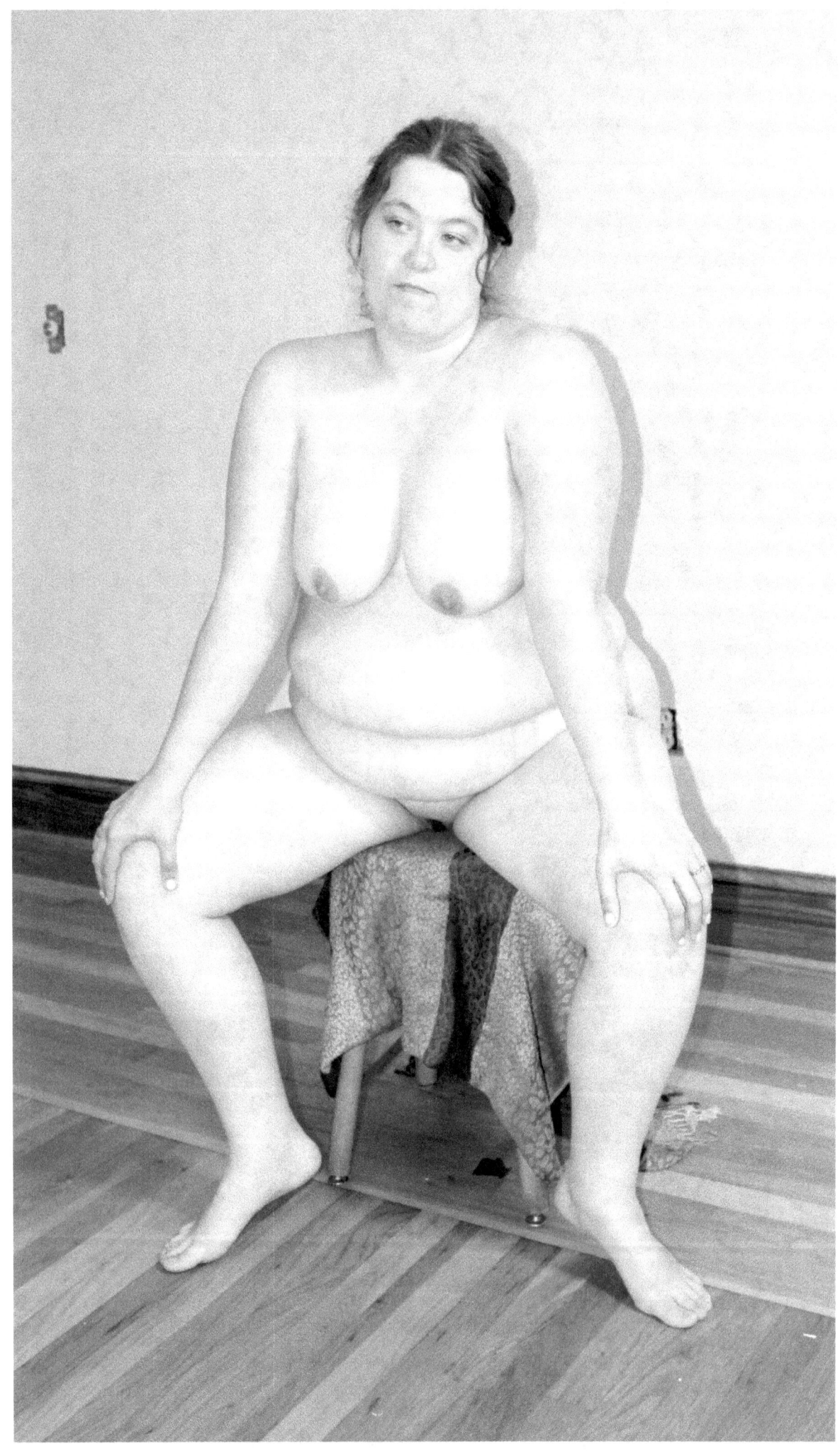

35

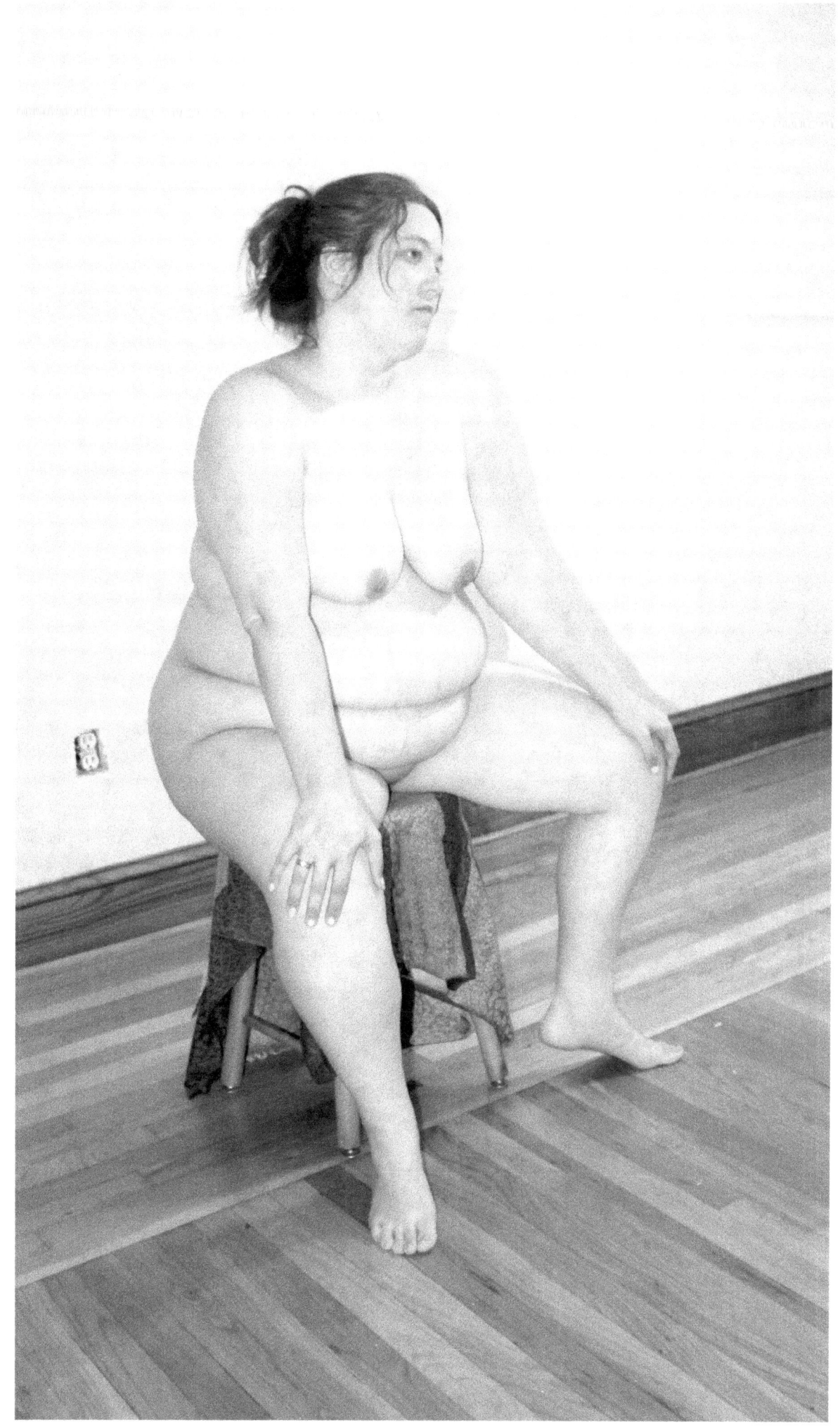

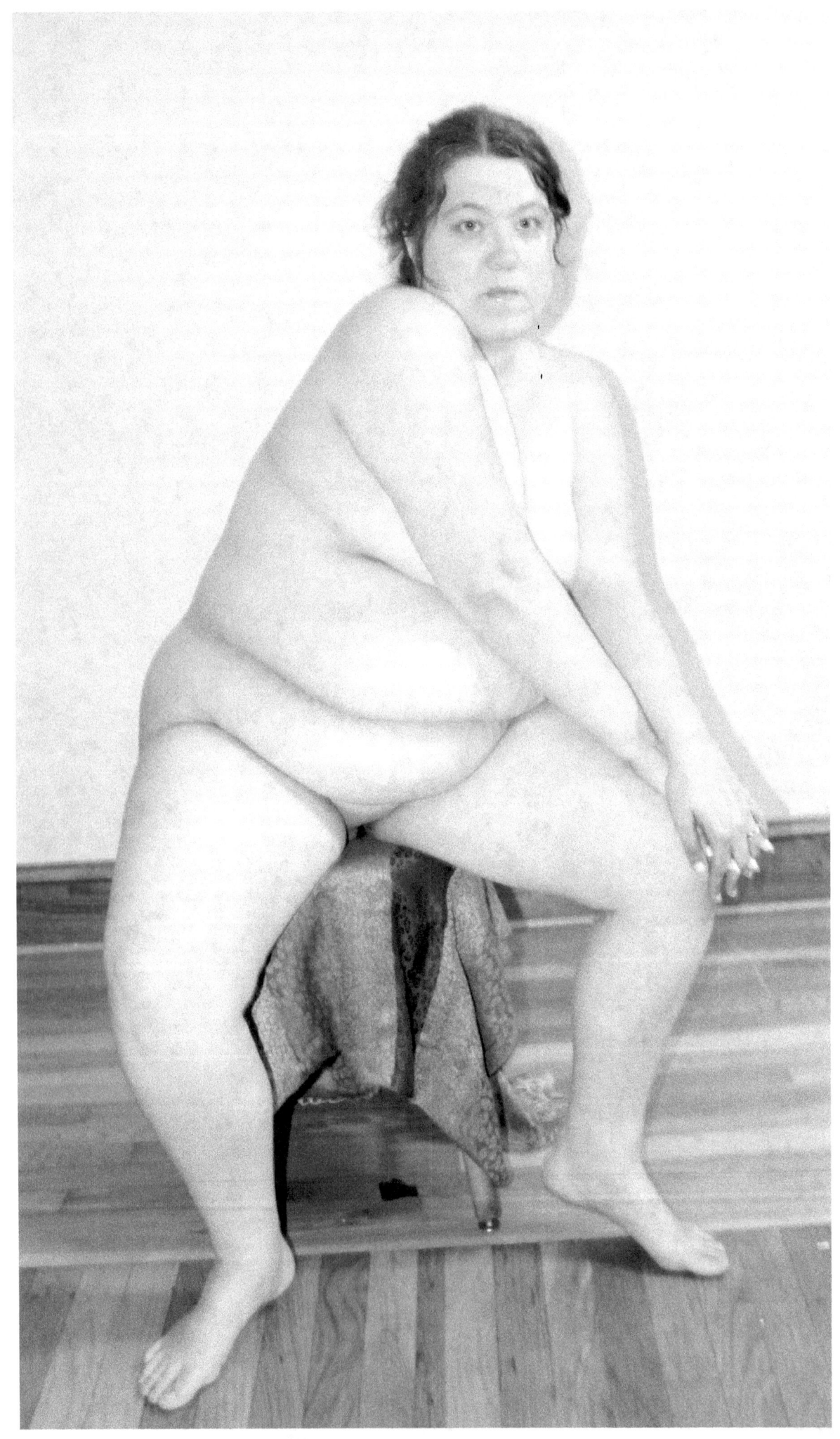

37

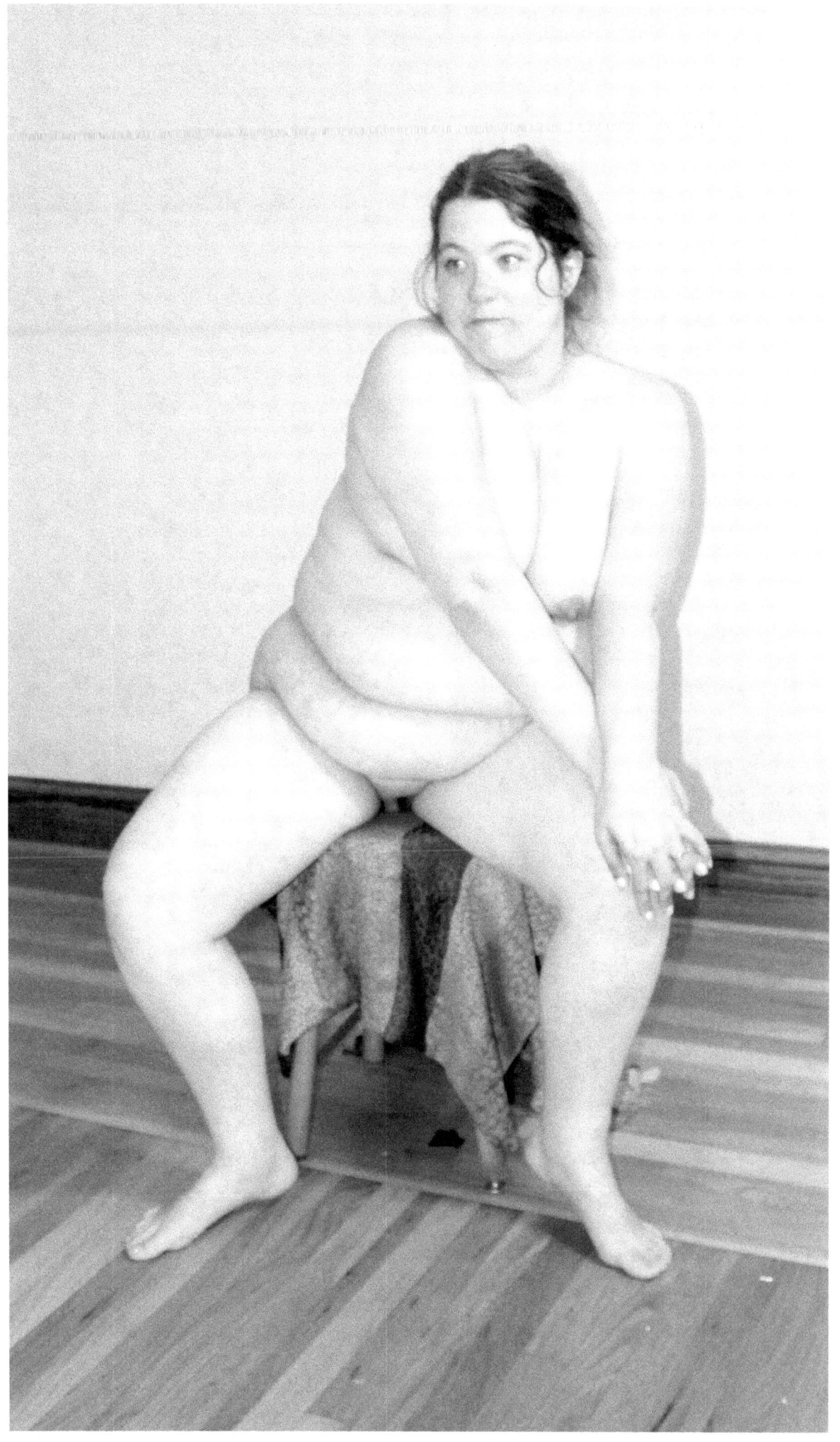

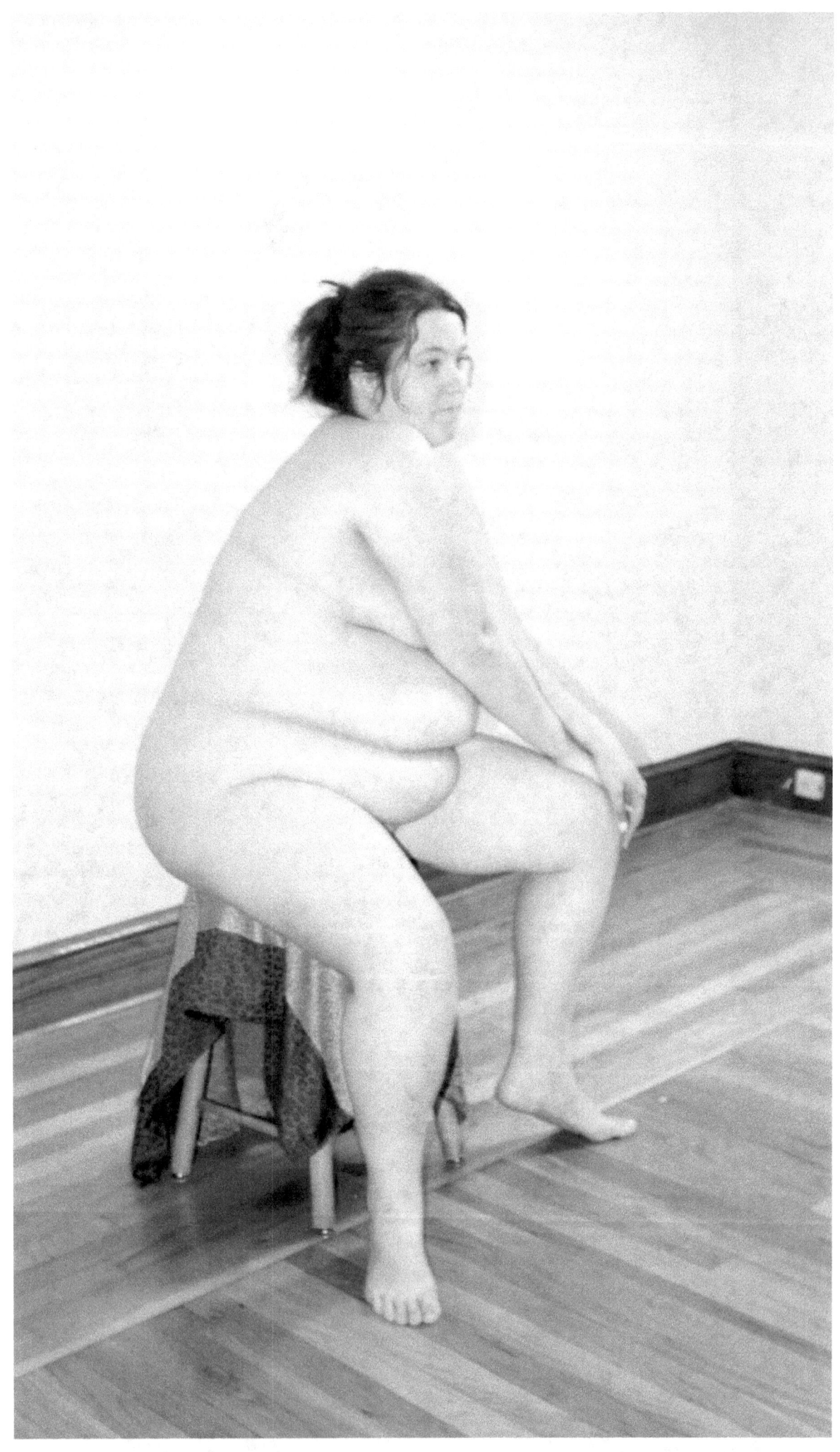

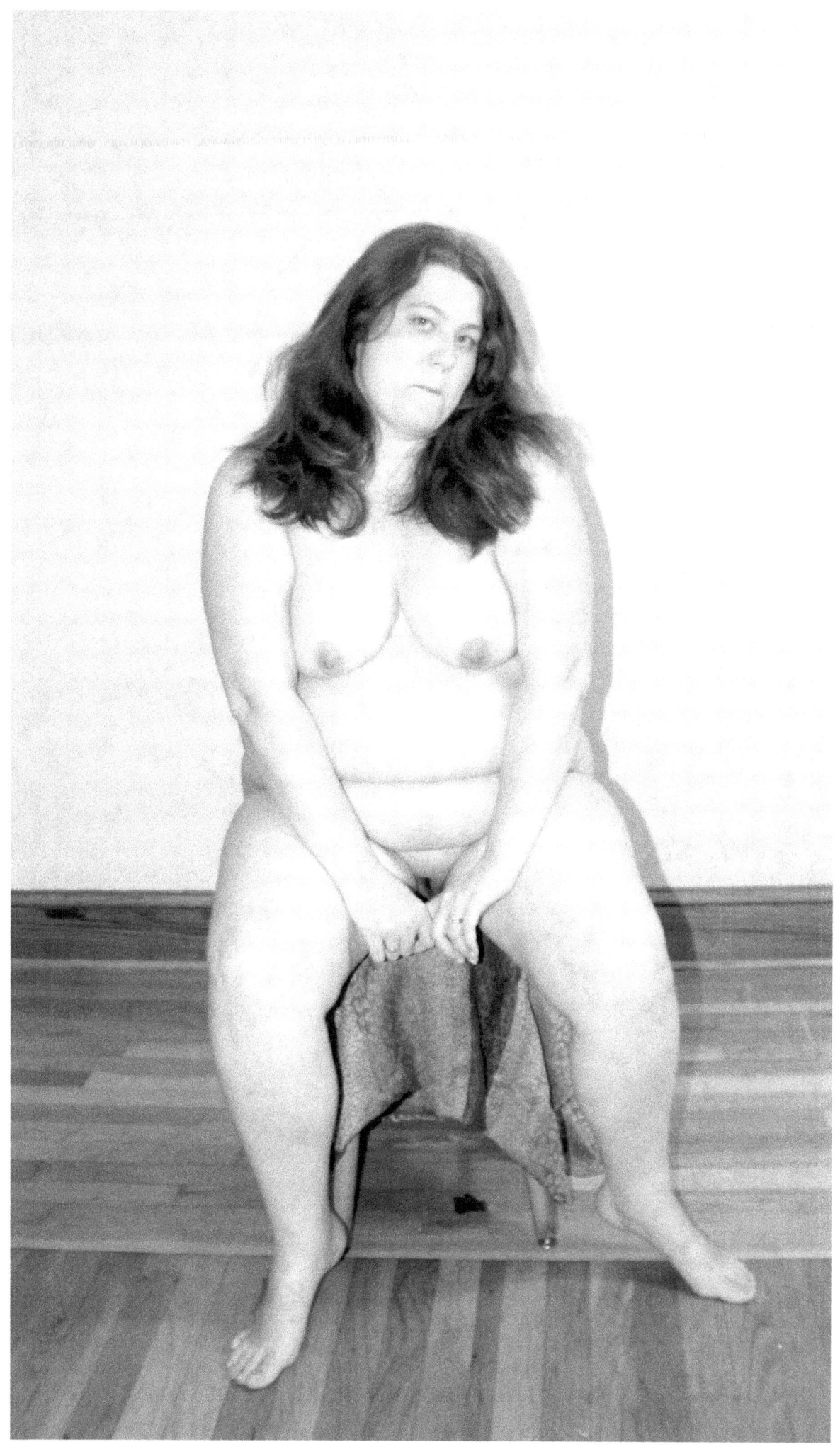

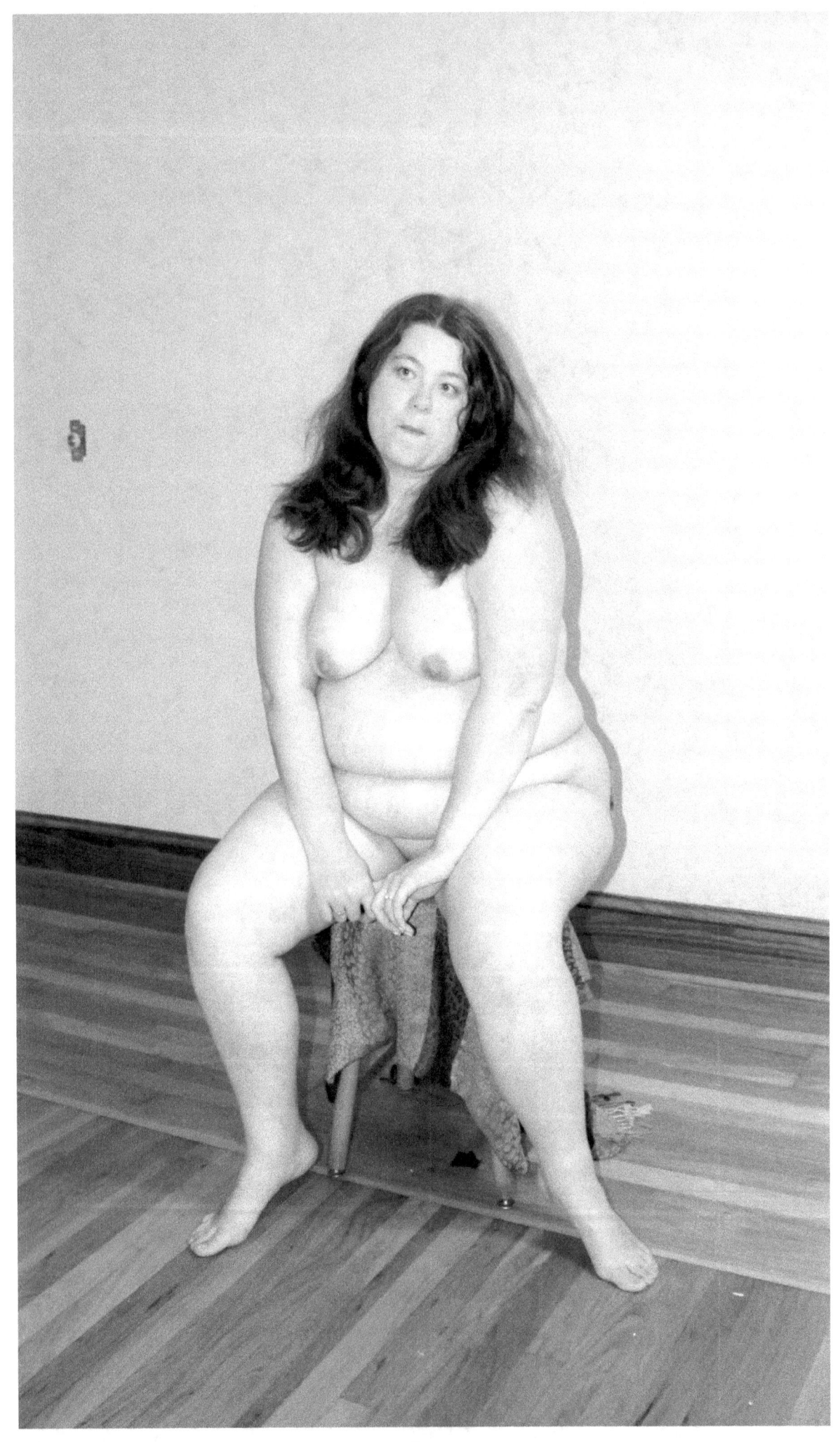

41

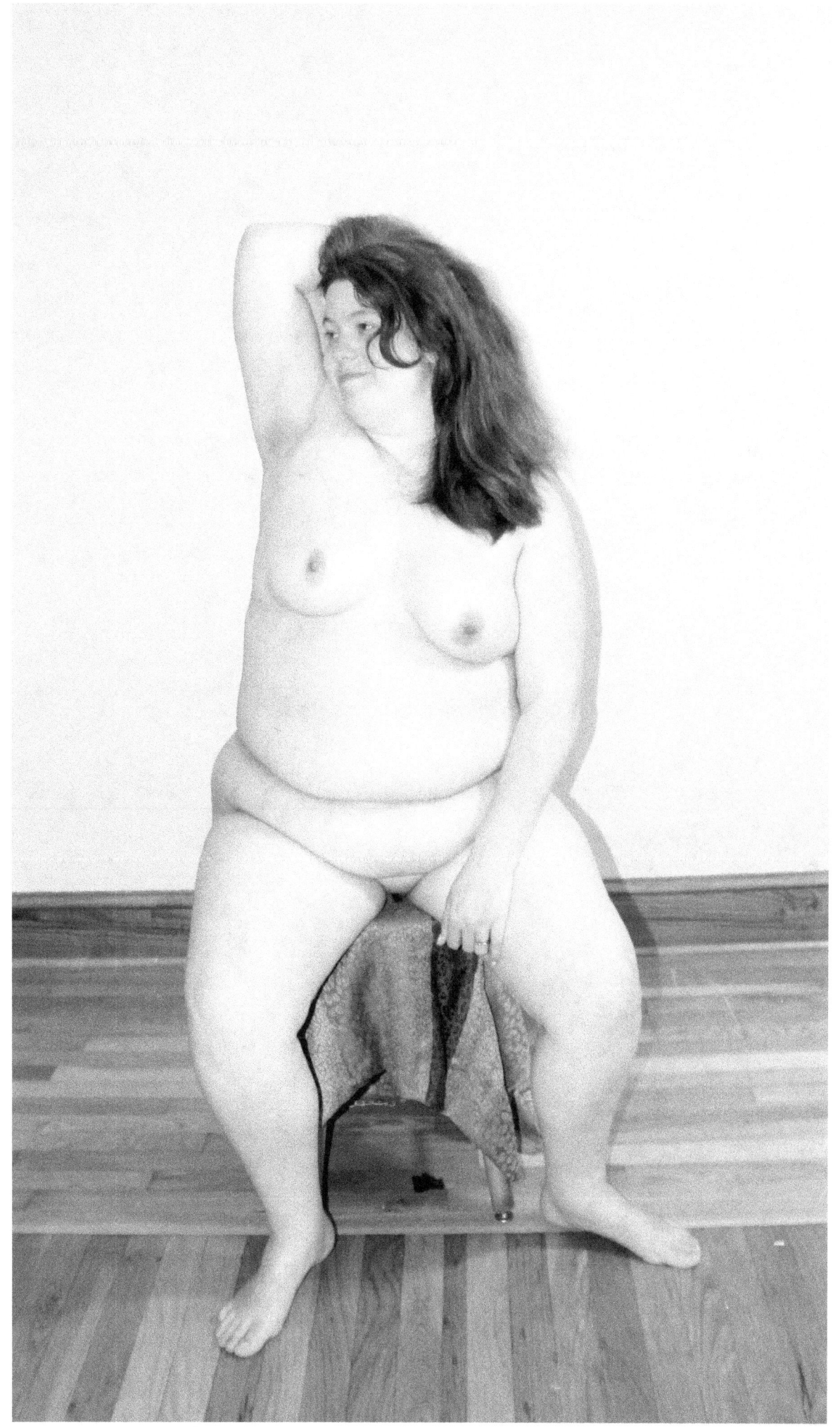

42

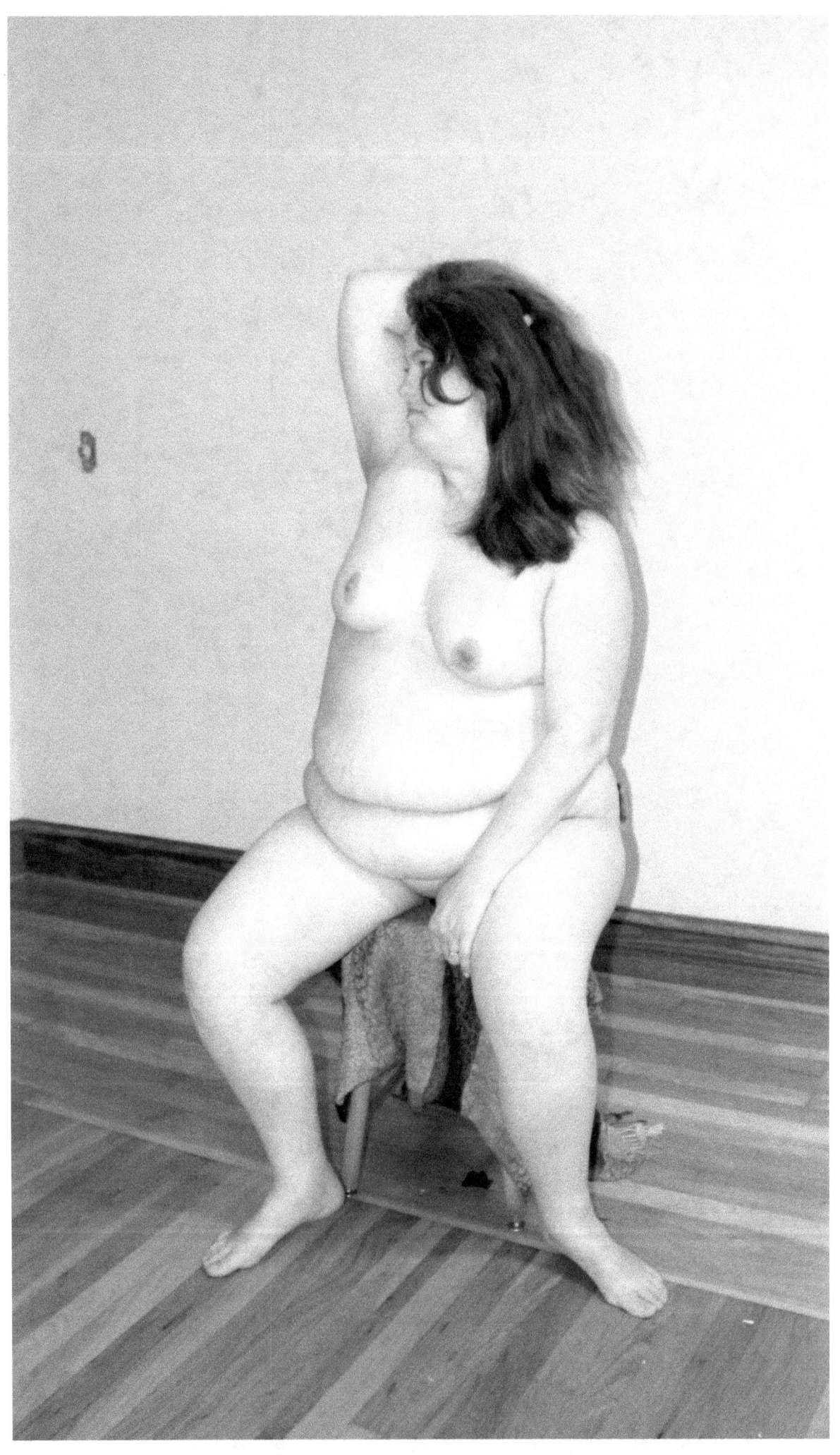

43

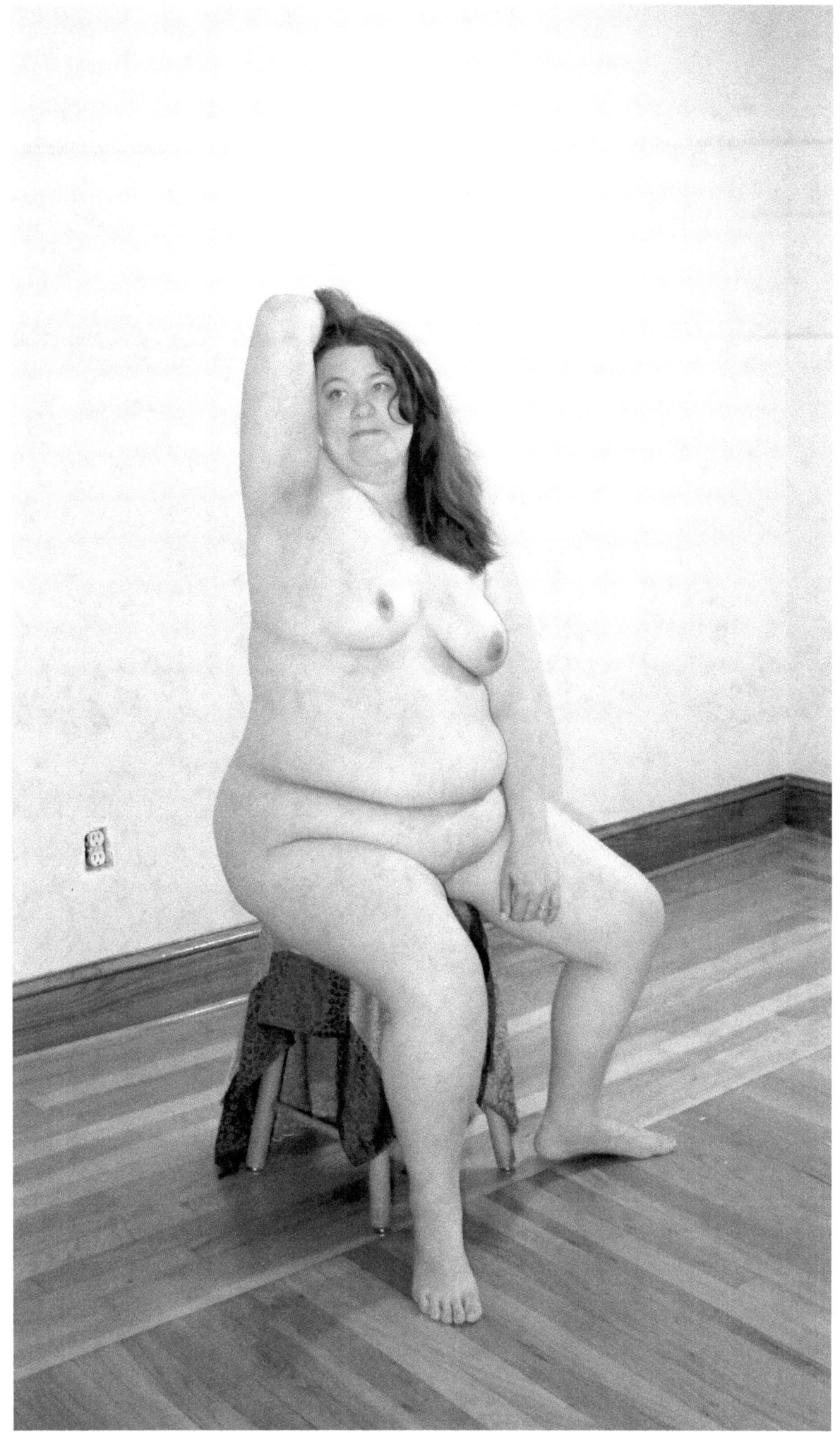

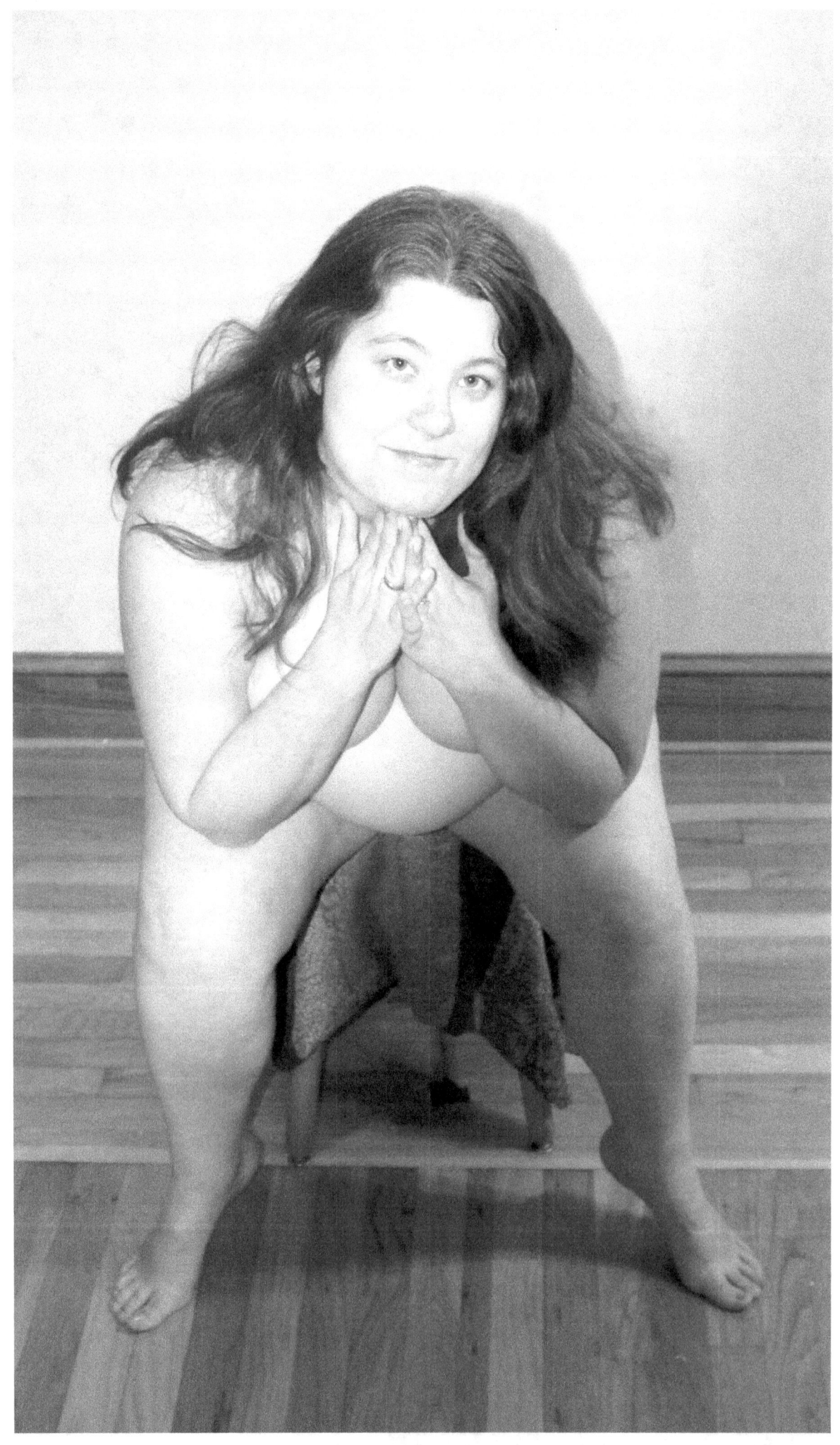

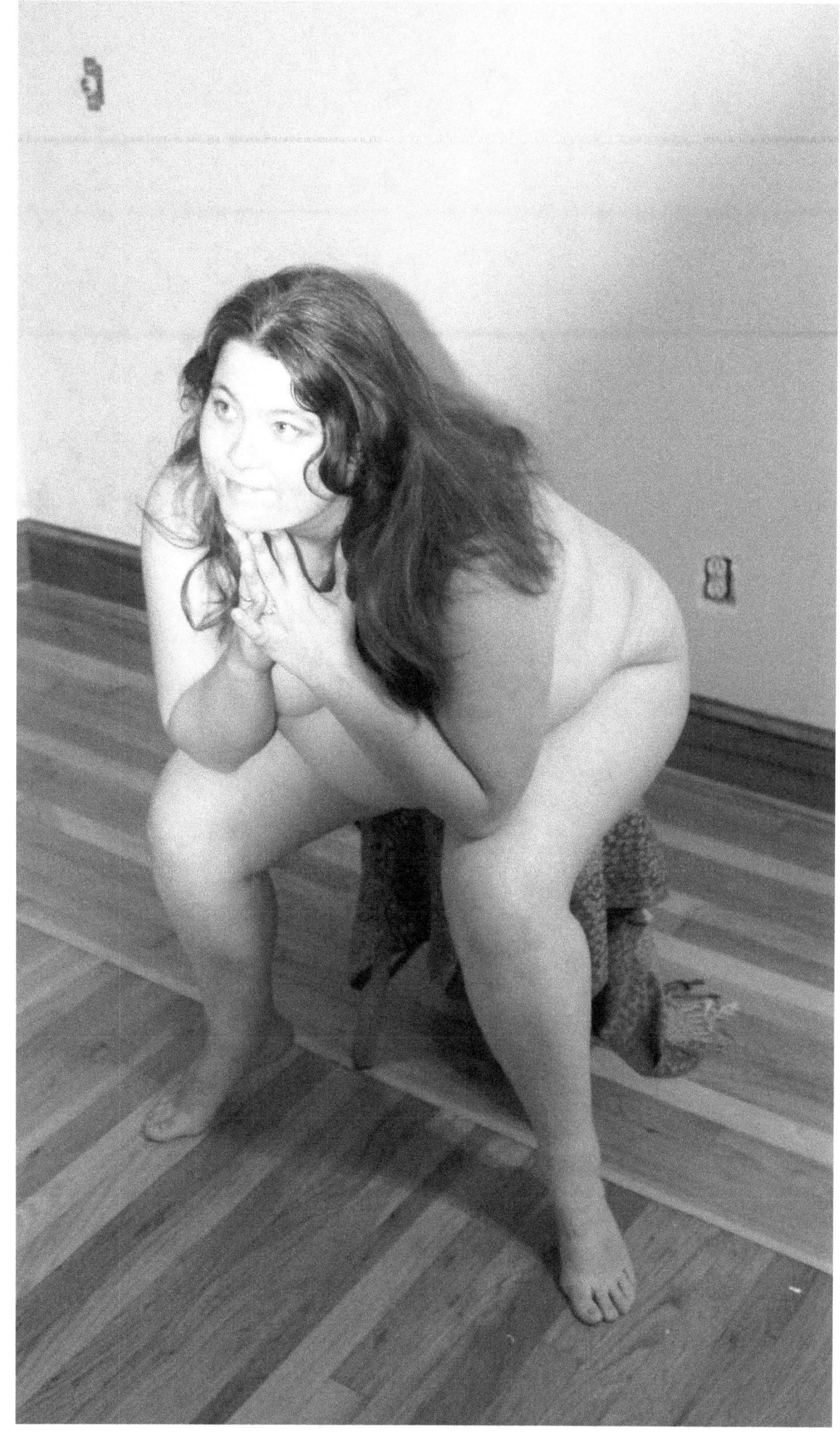

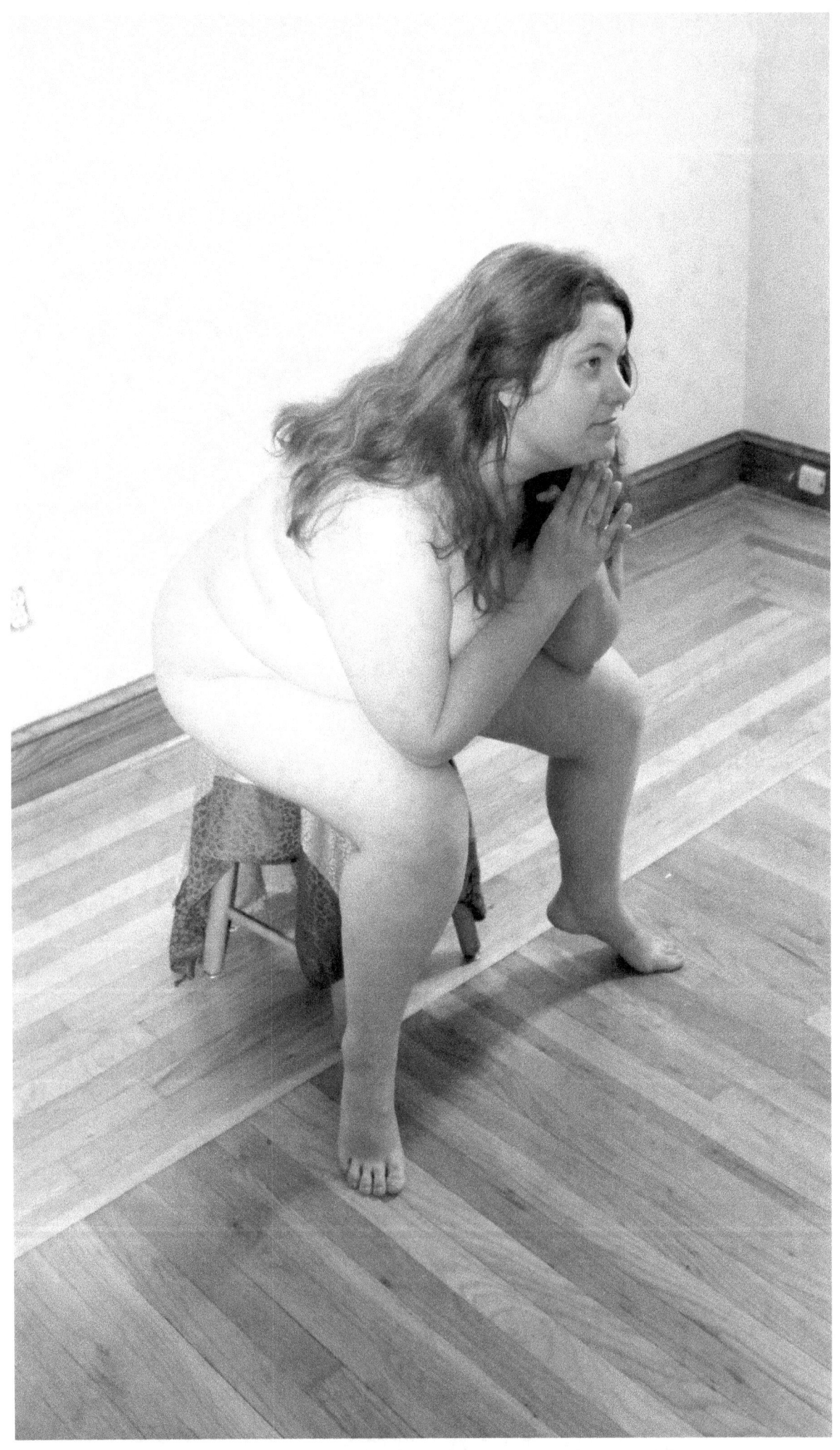

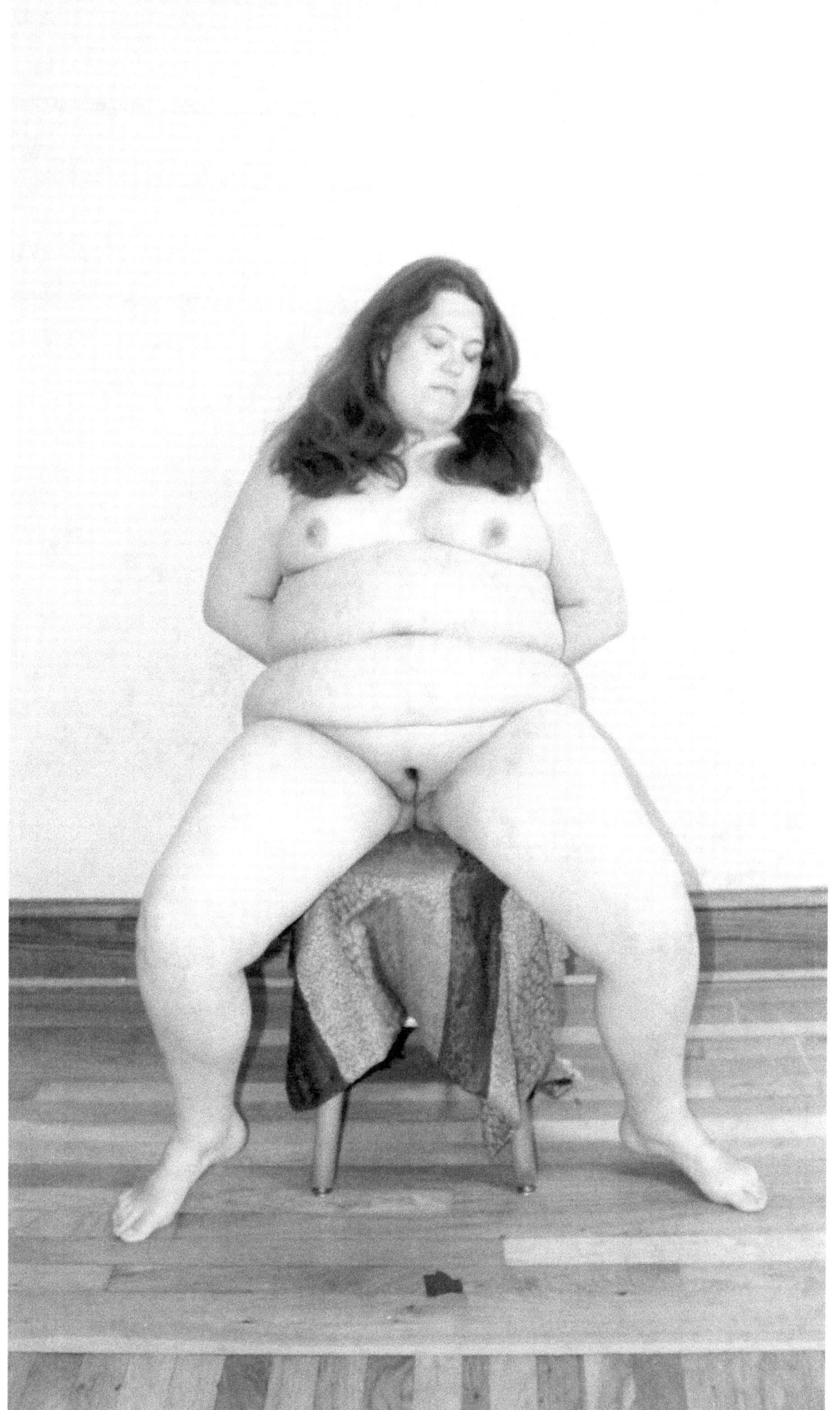

48

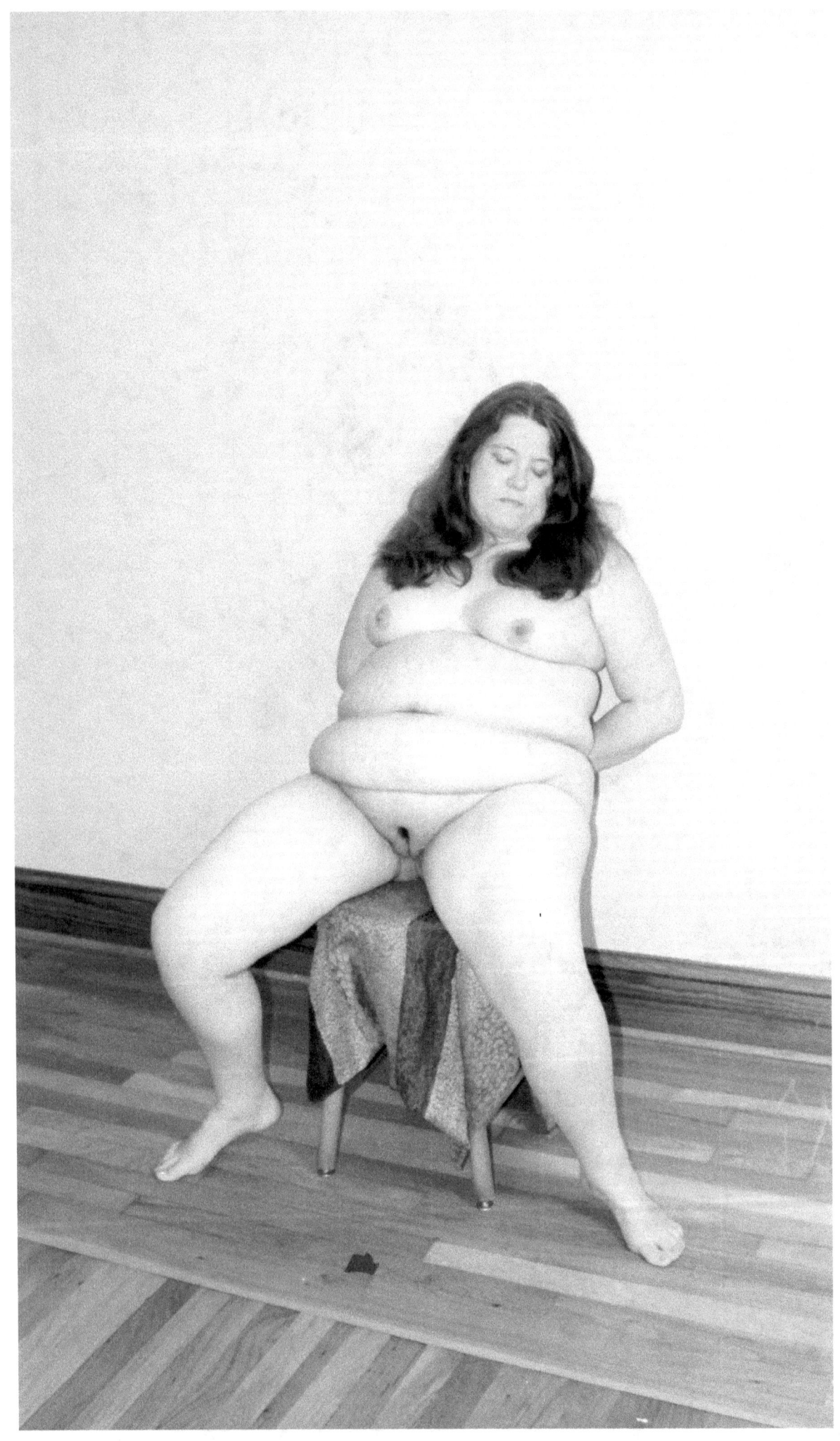

49

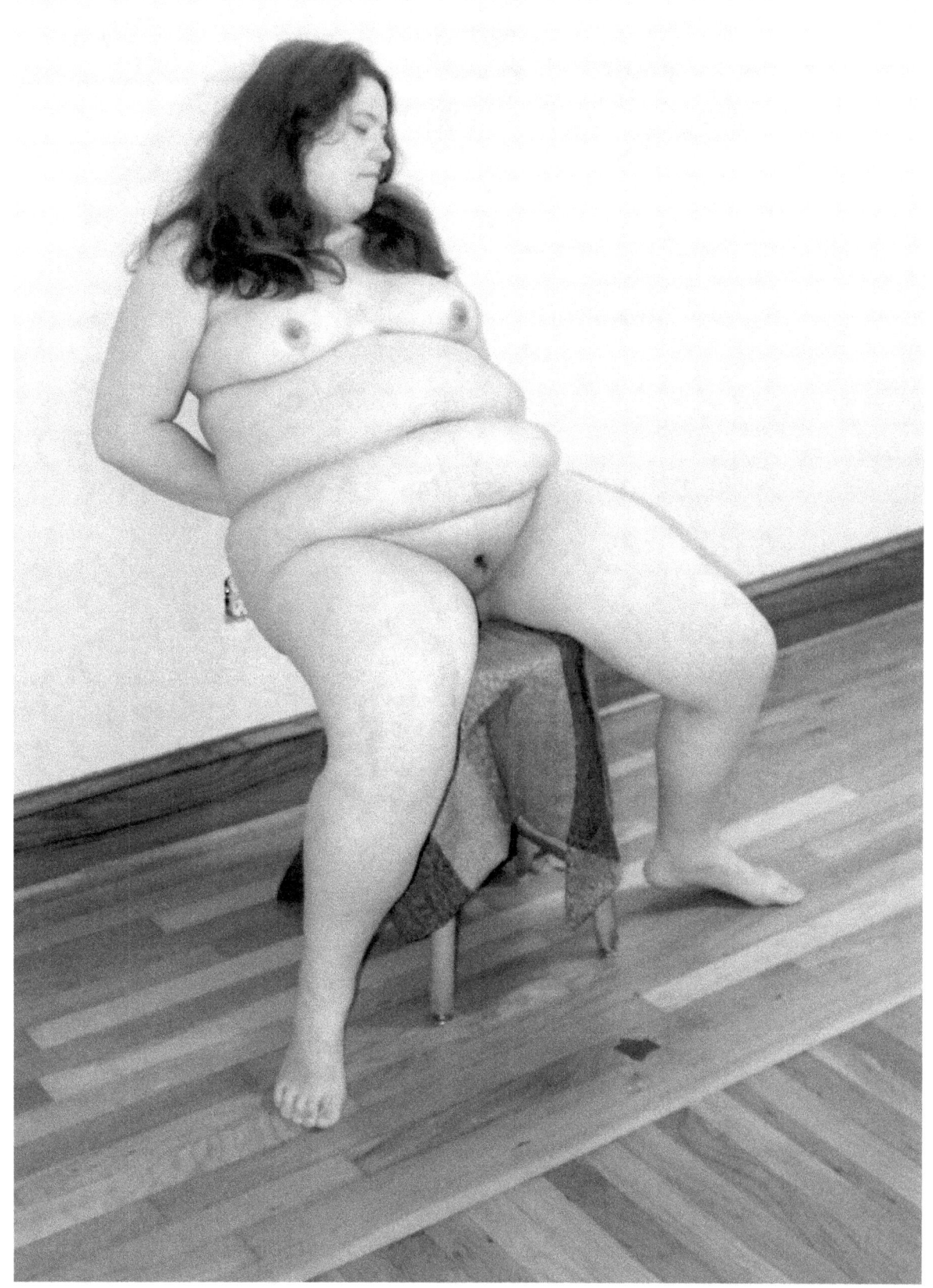

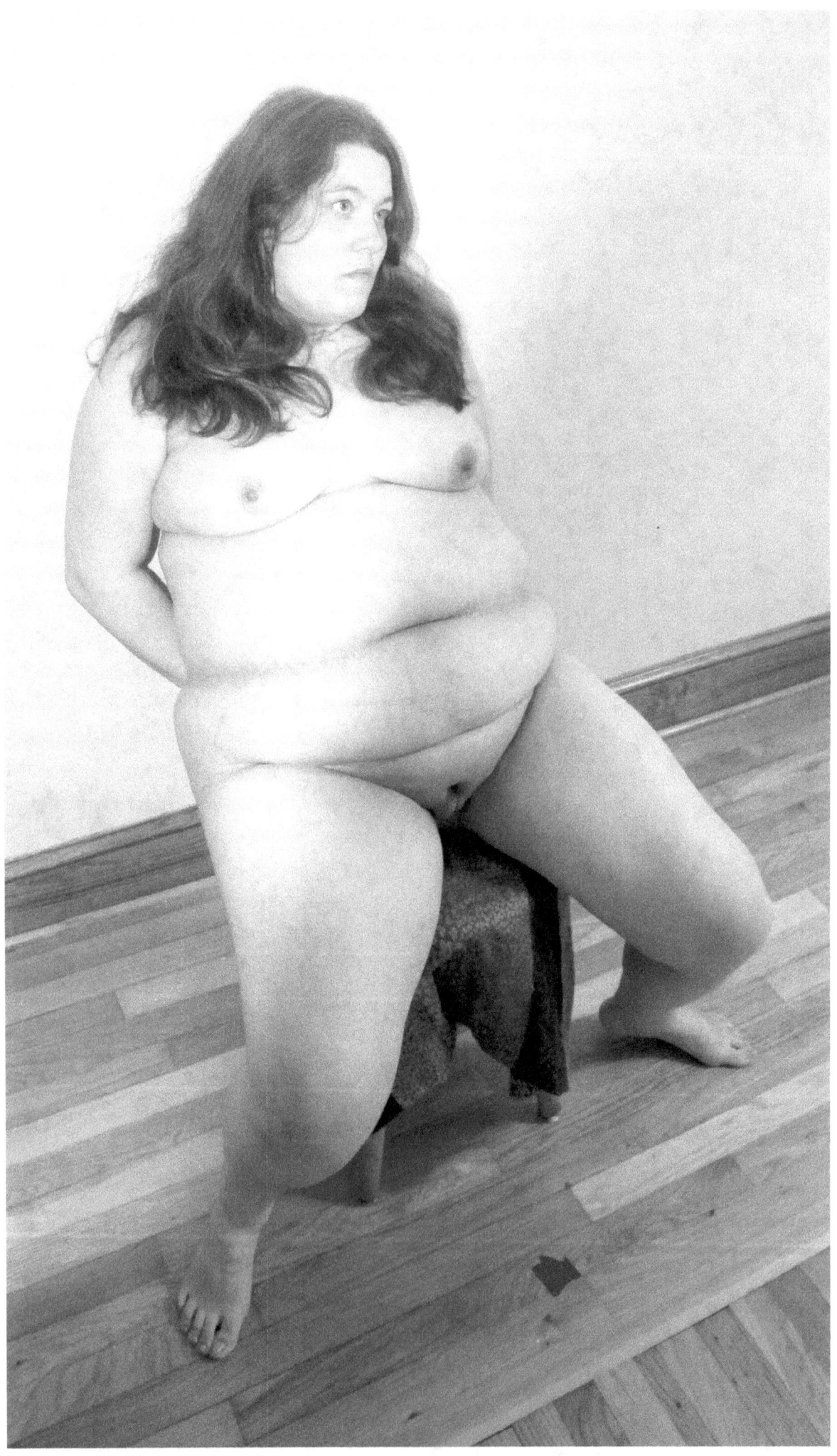

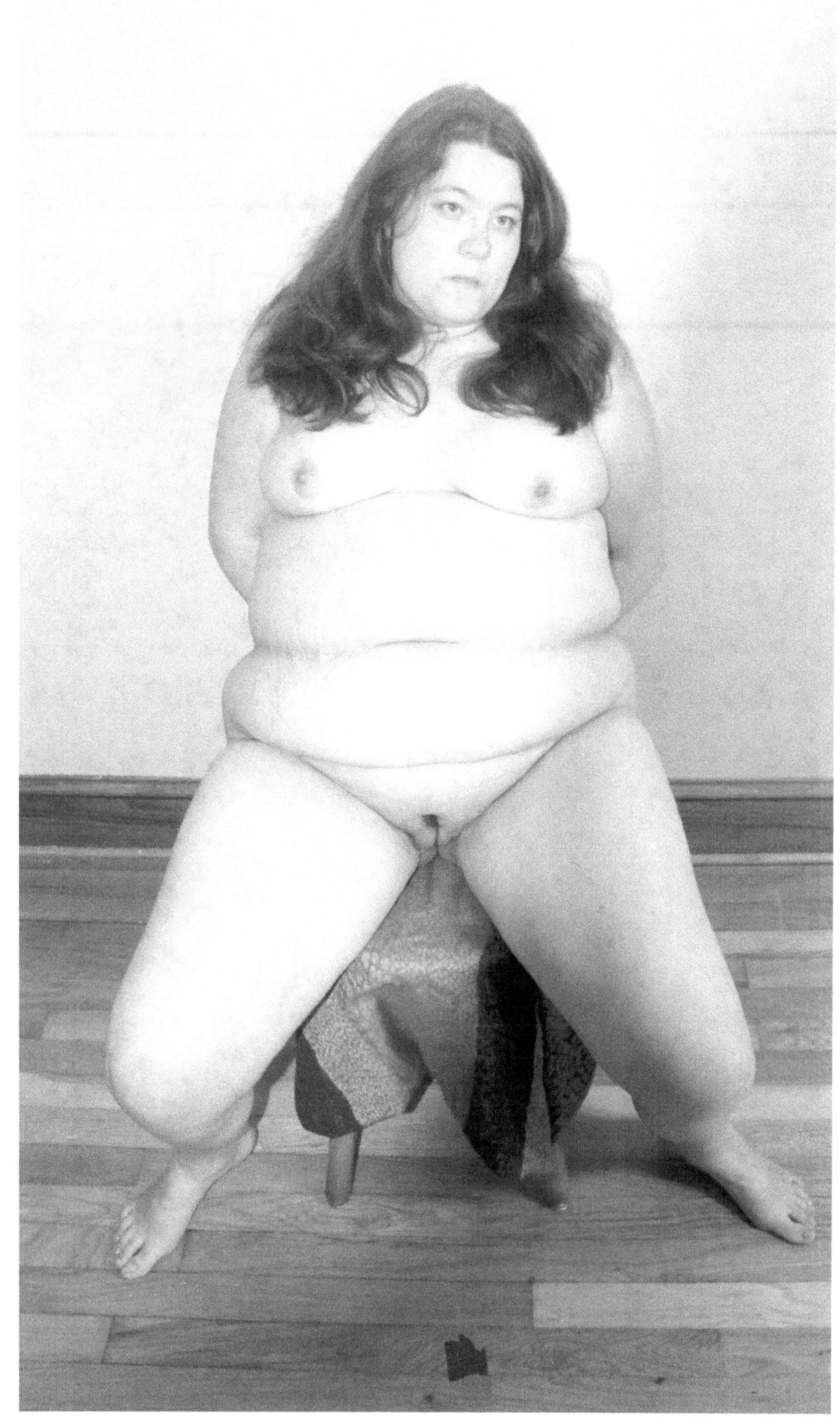

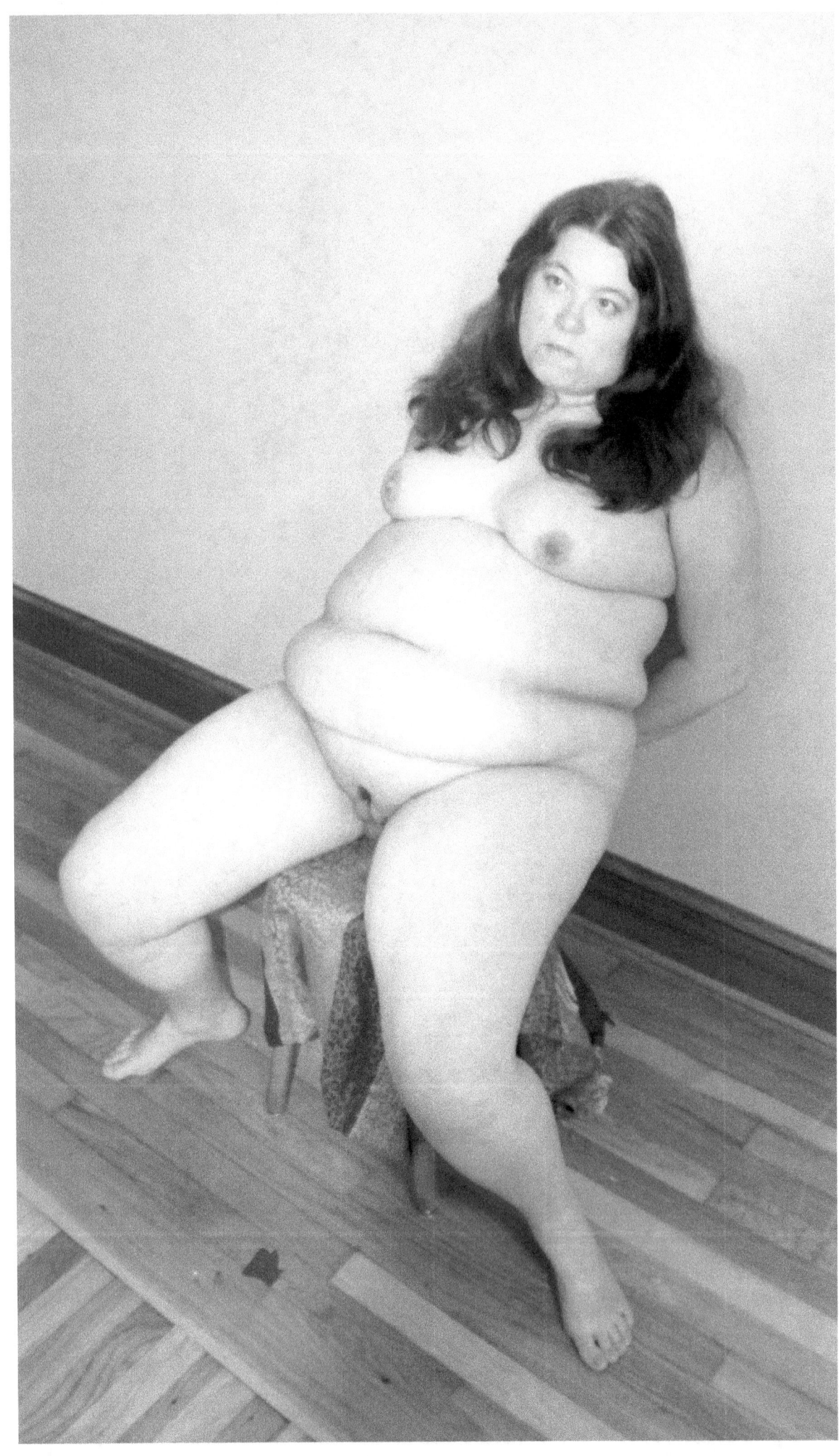

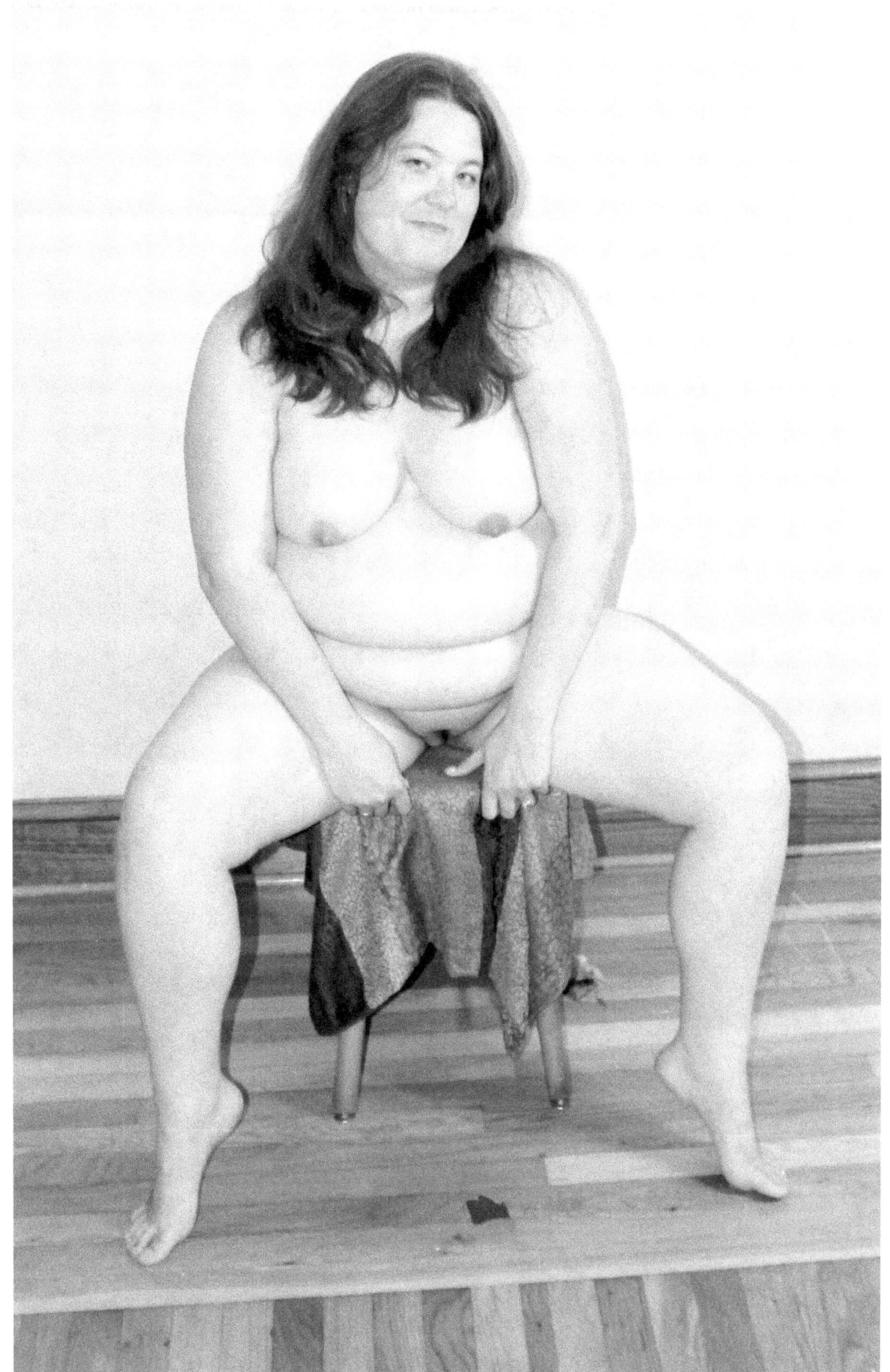

54

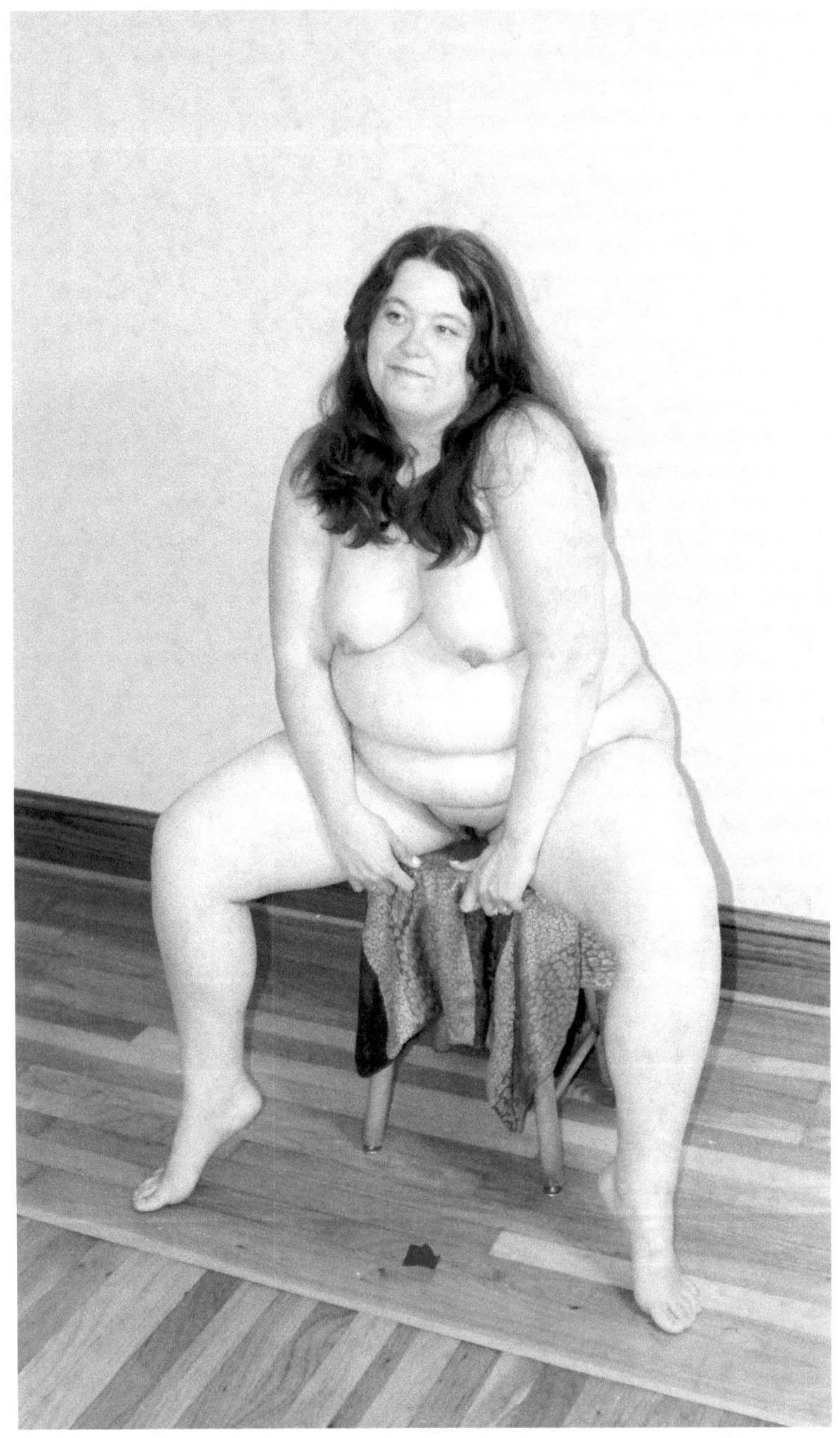

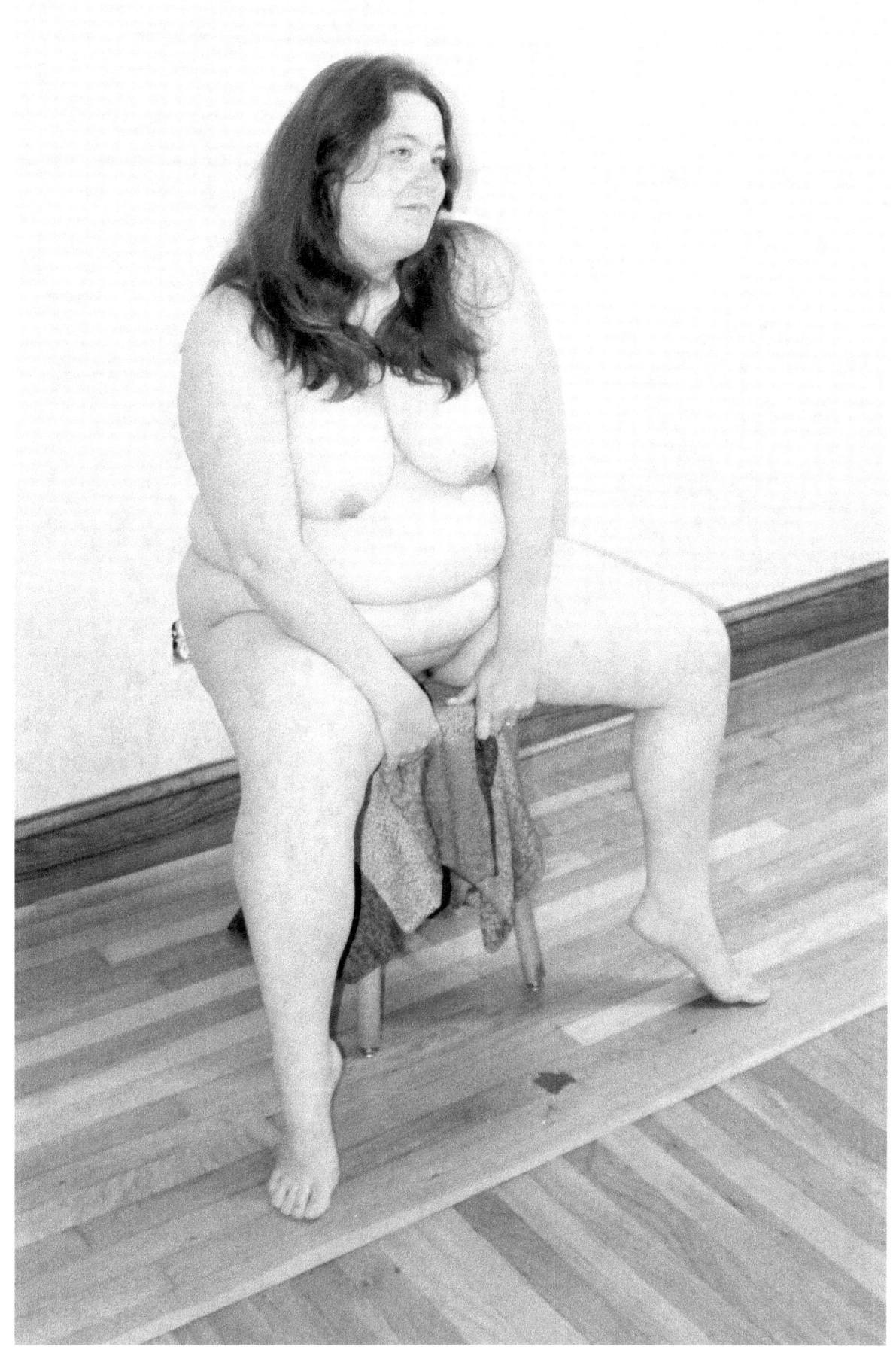

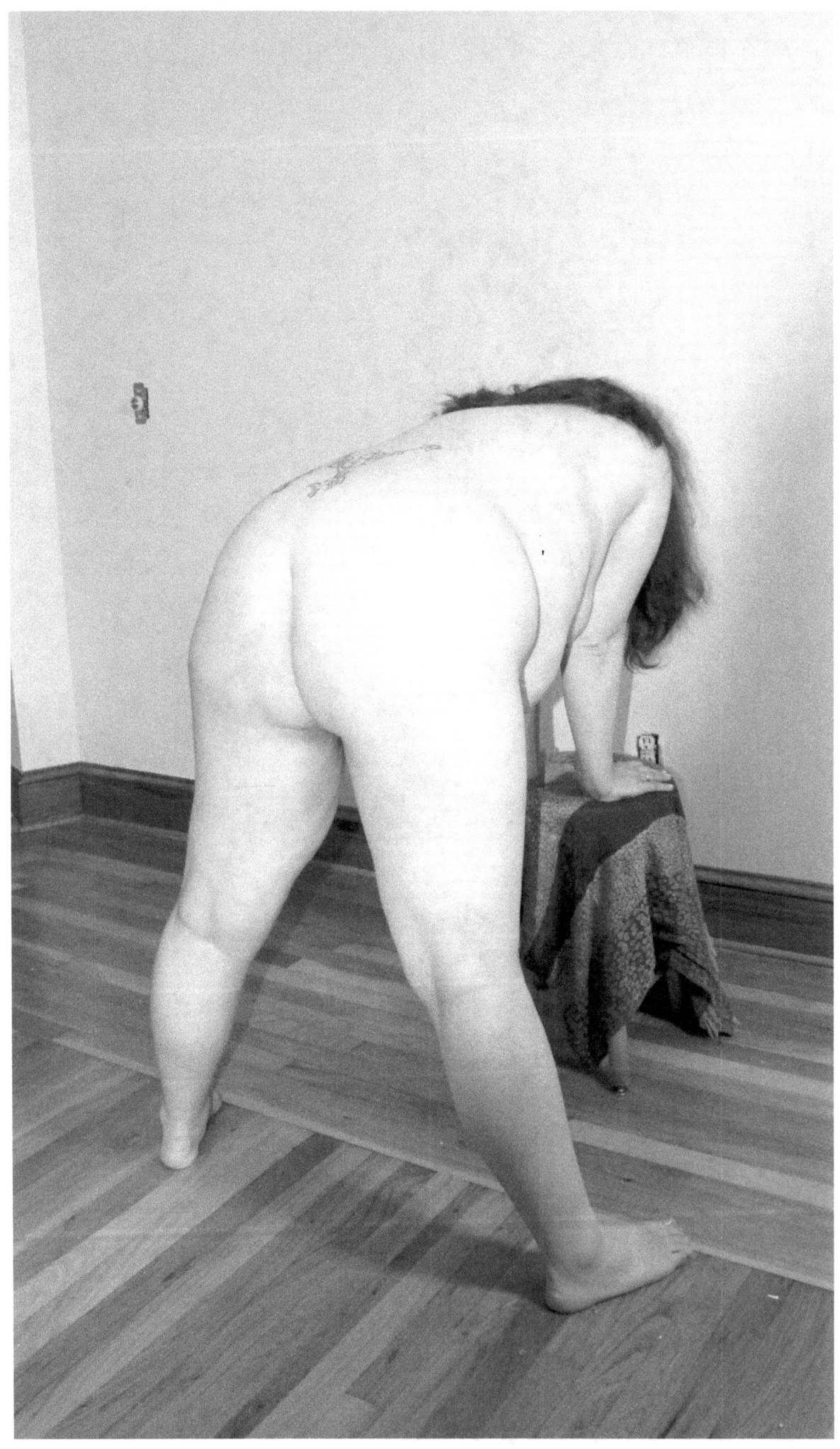

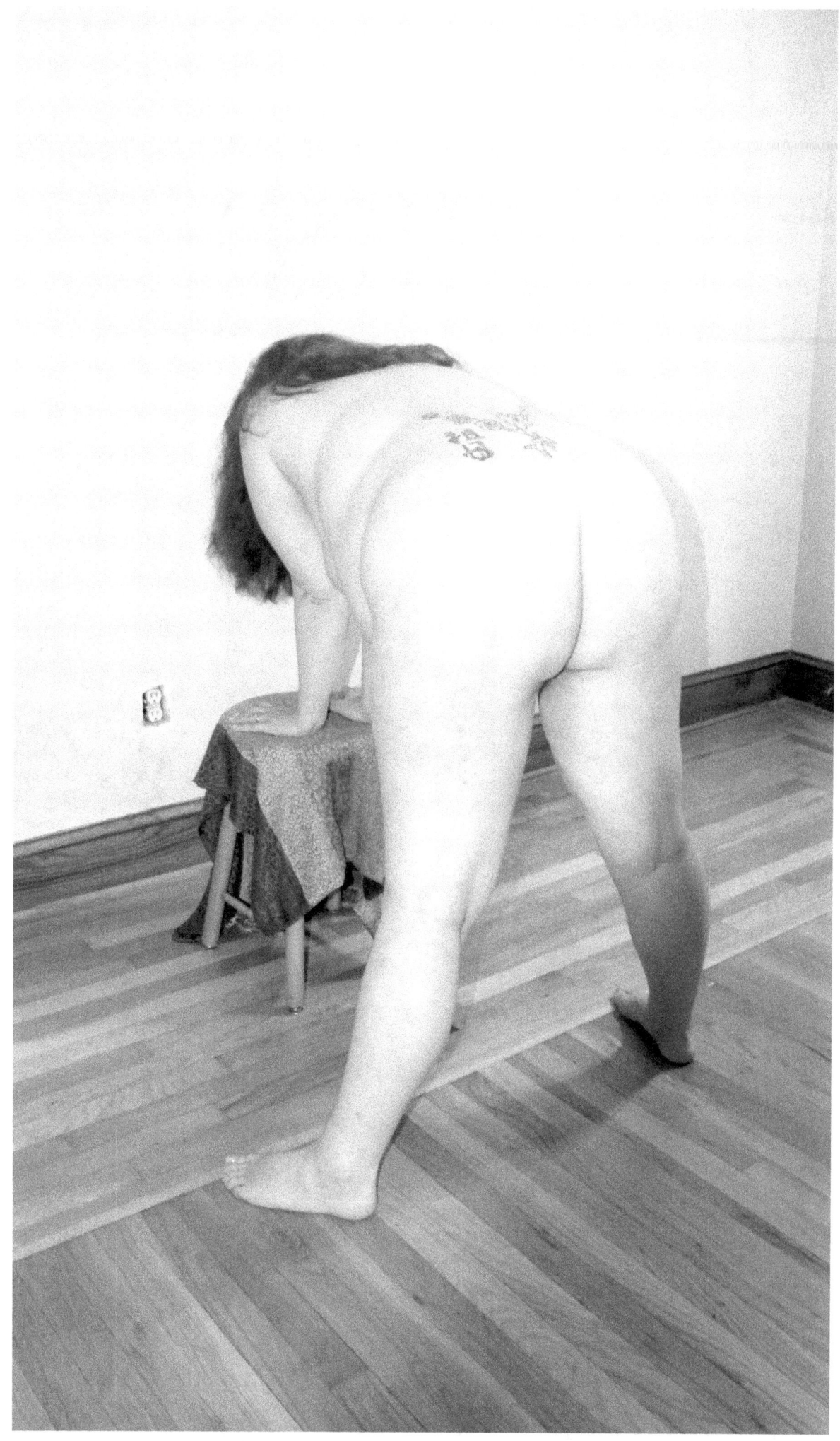

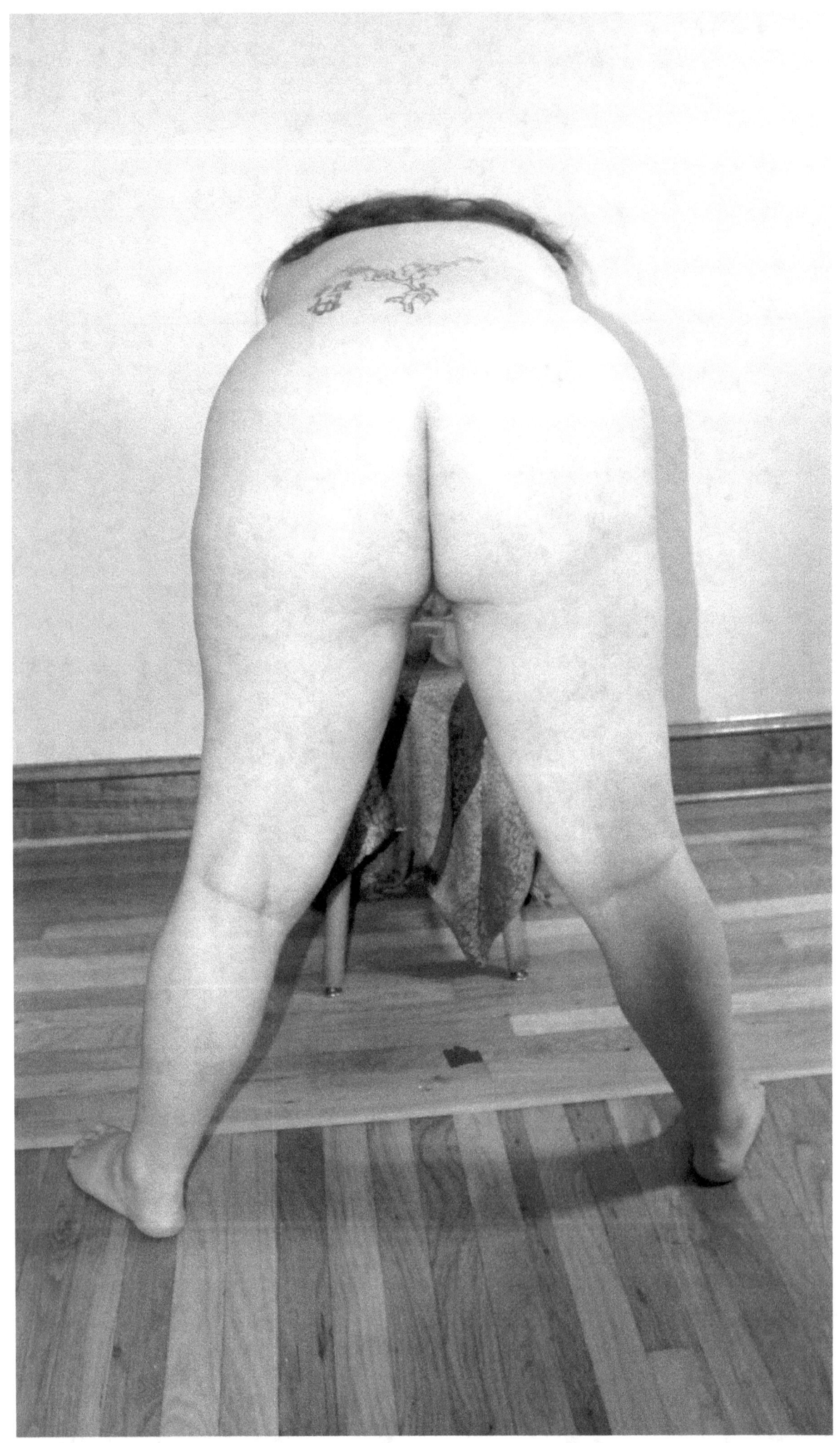

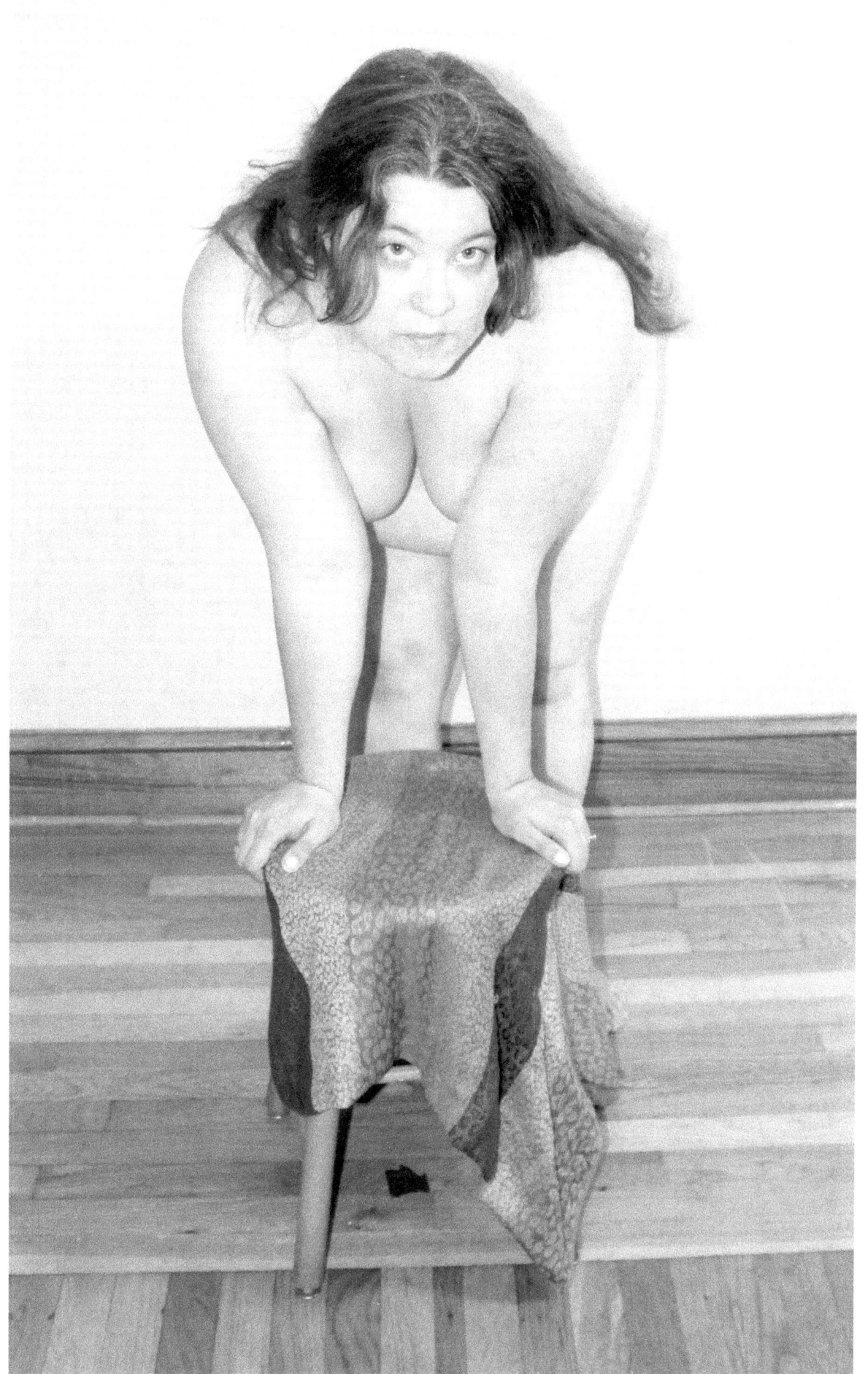

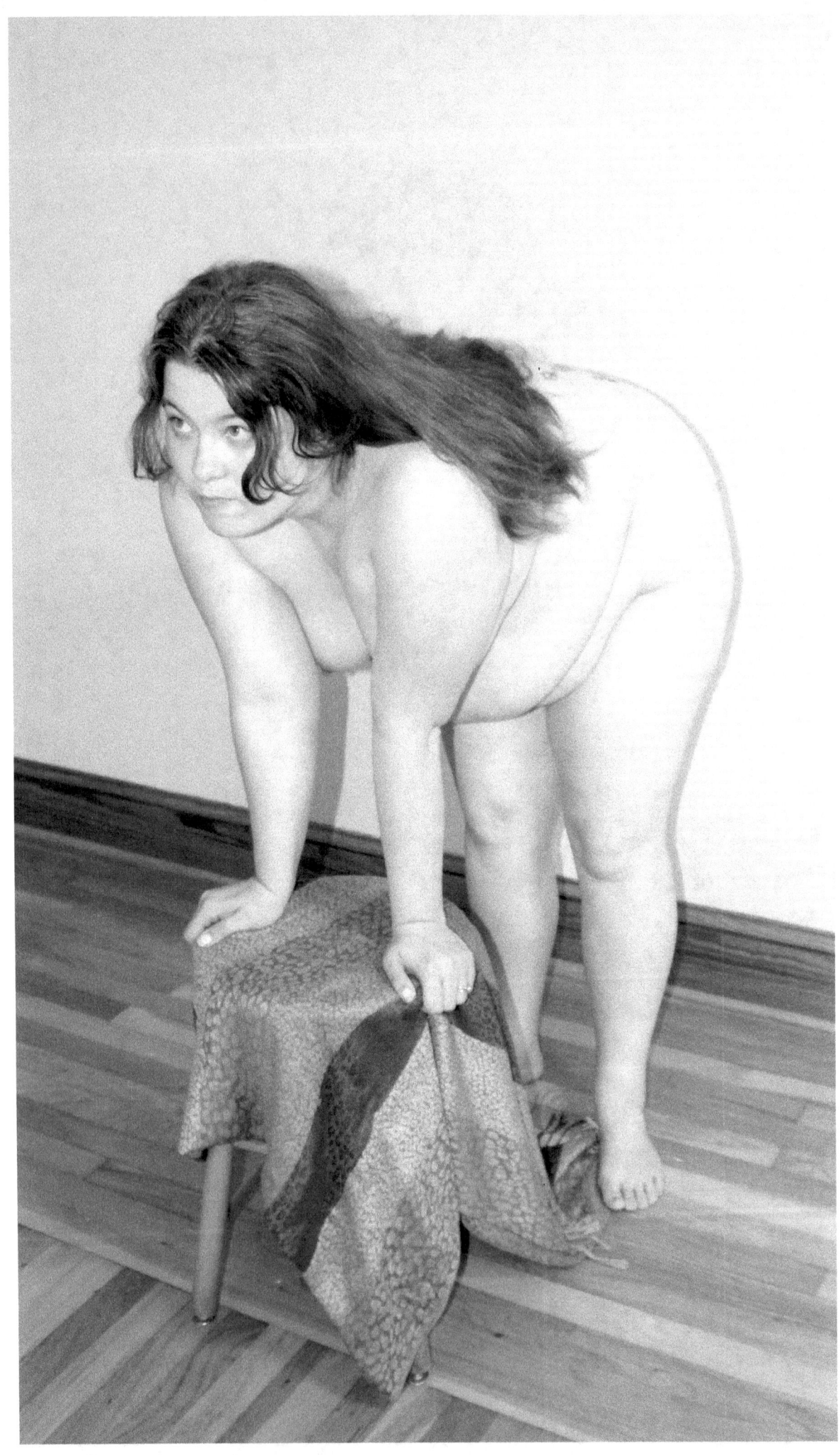

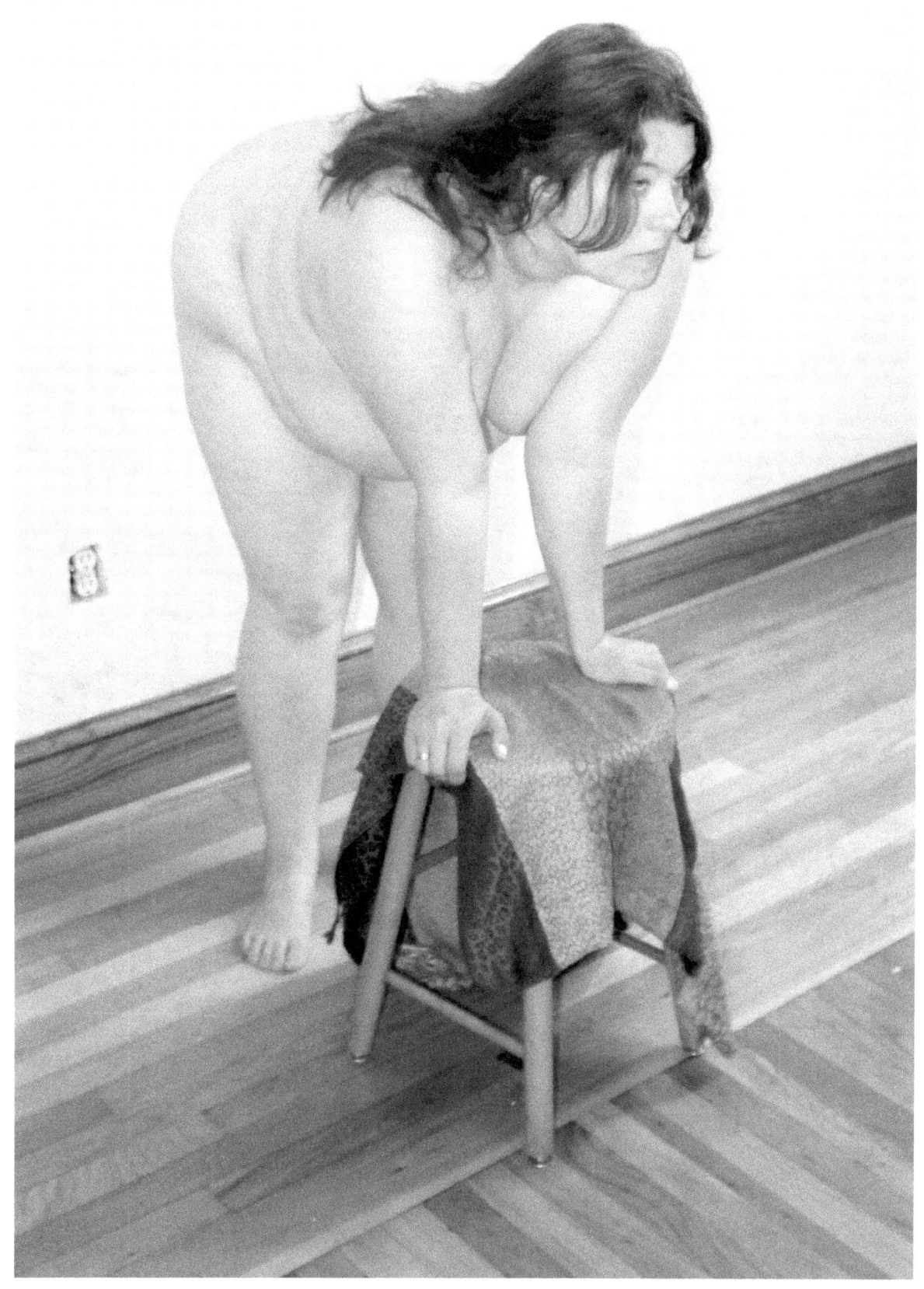

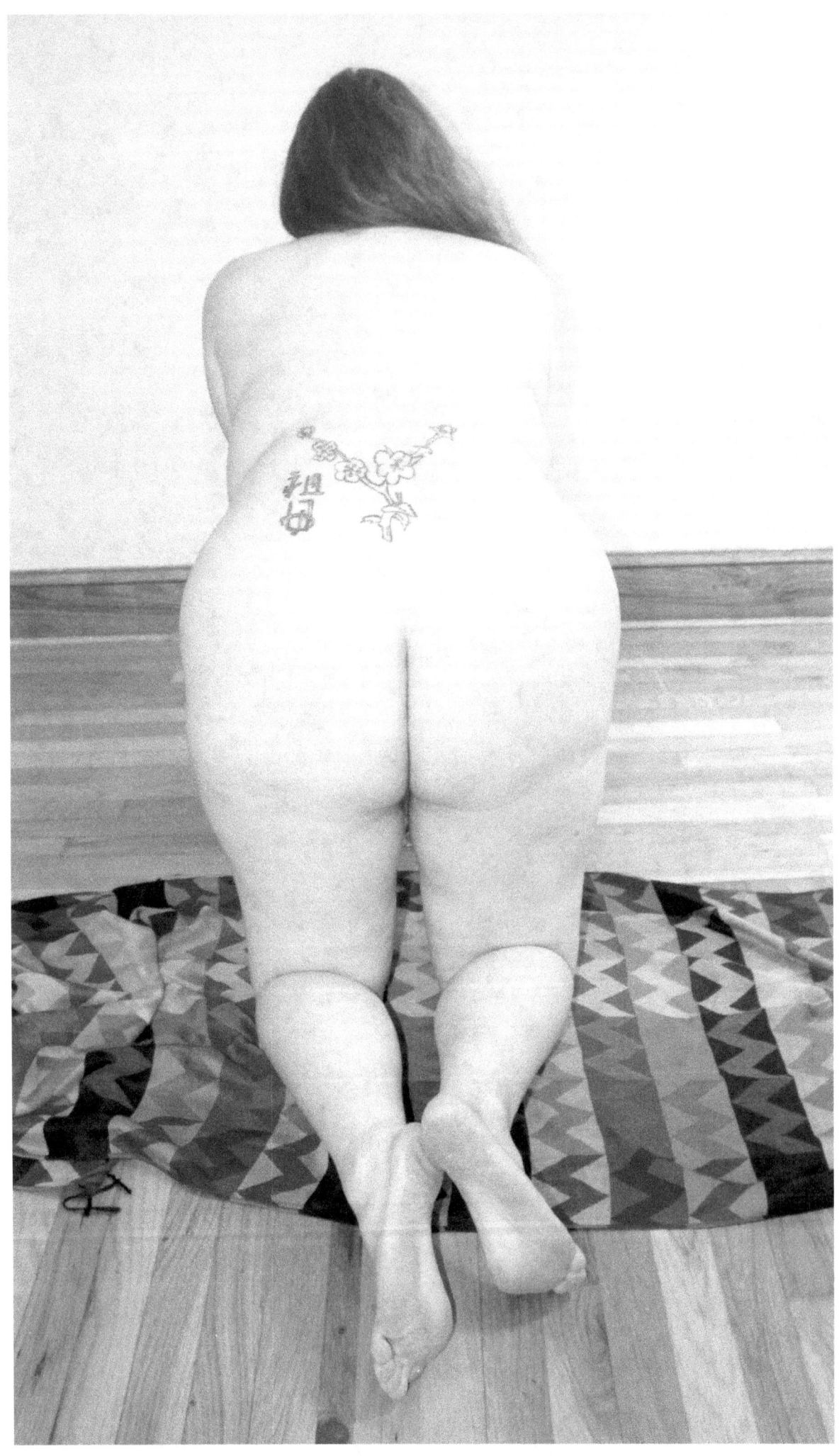

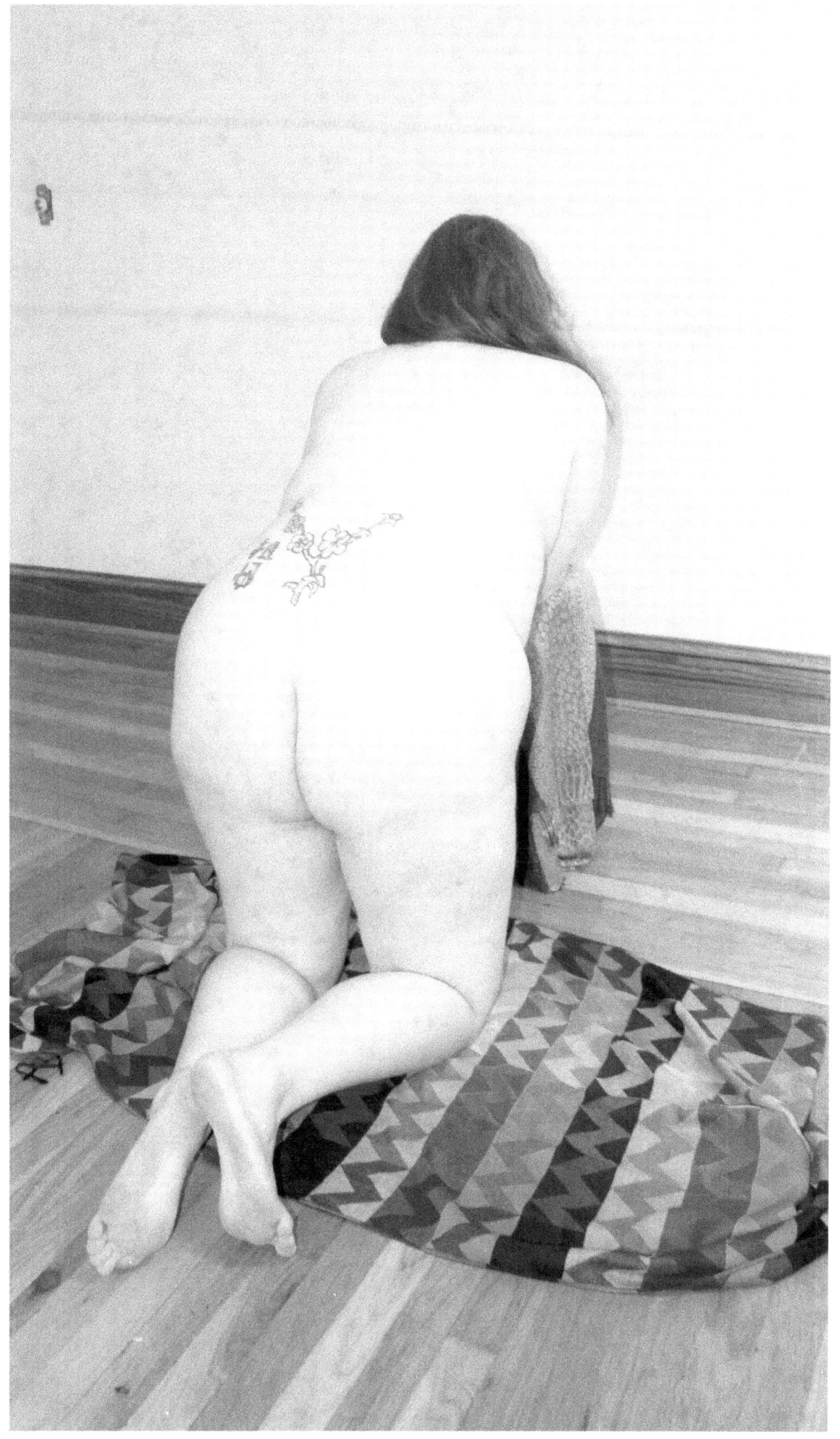

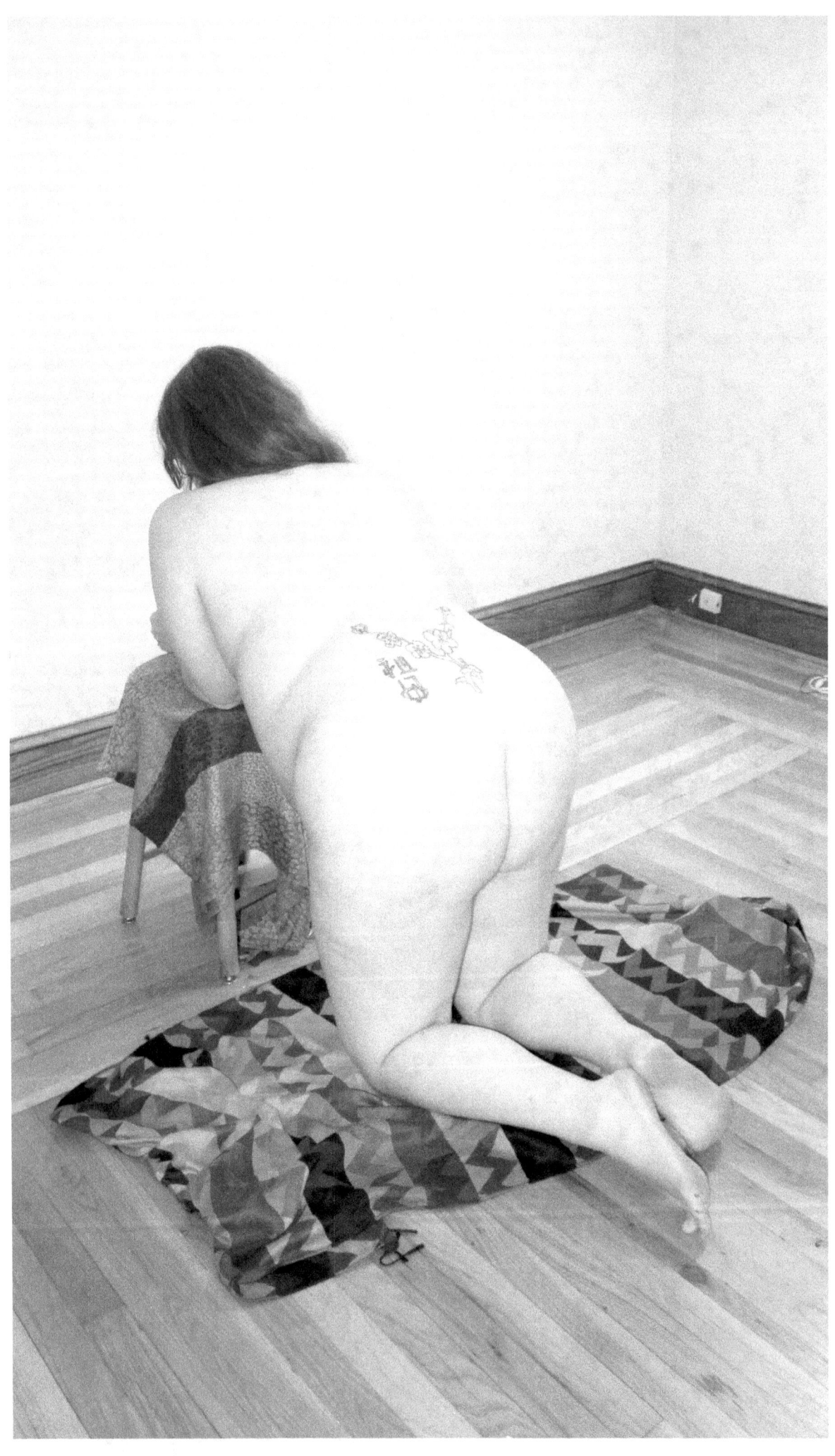

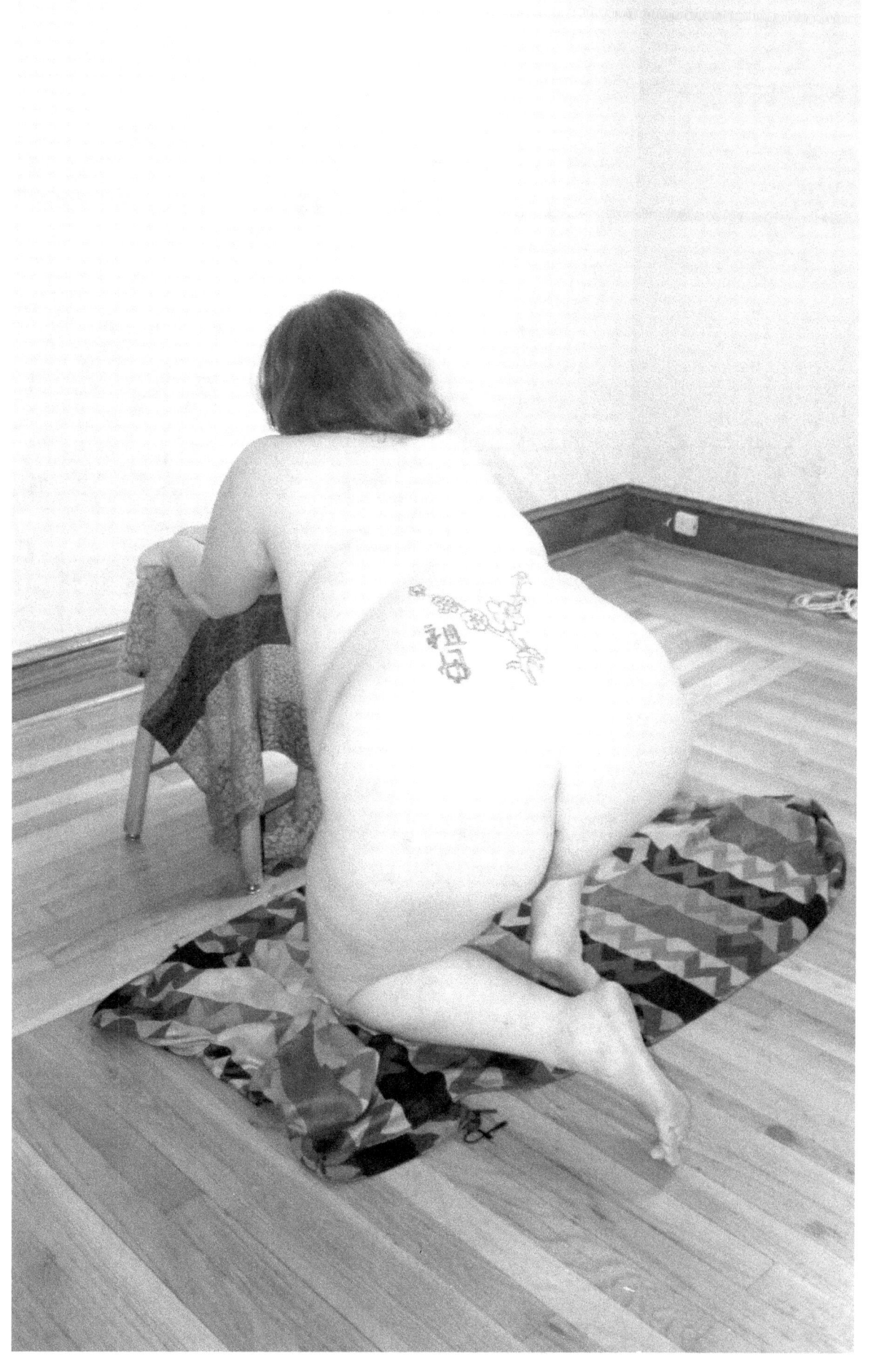

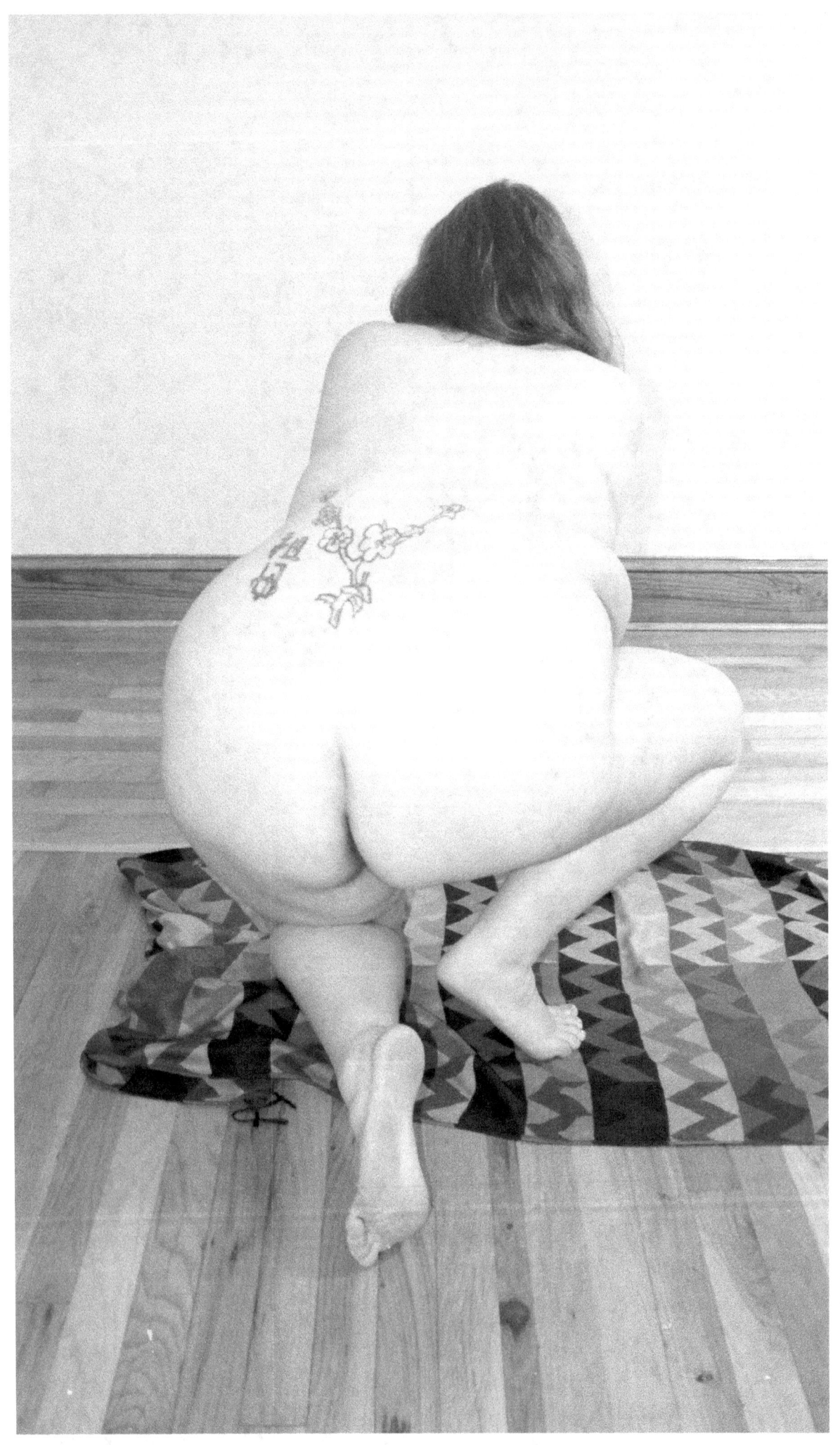

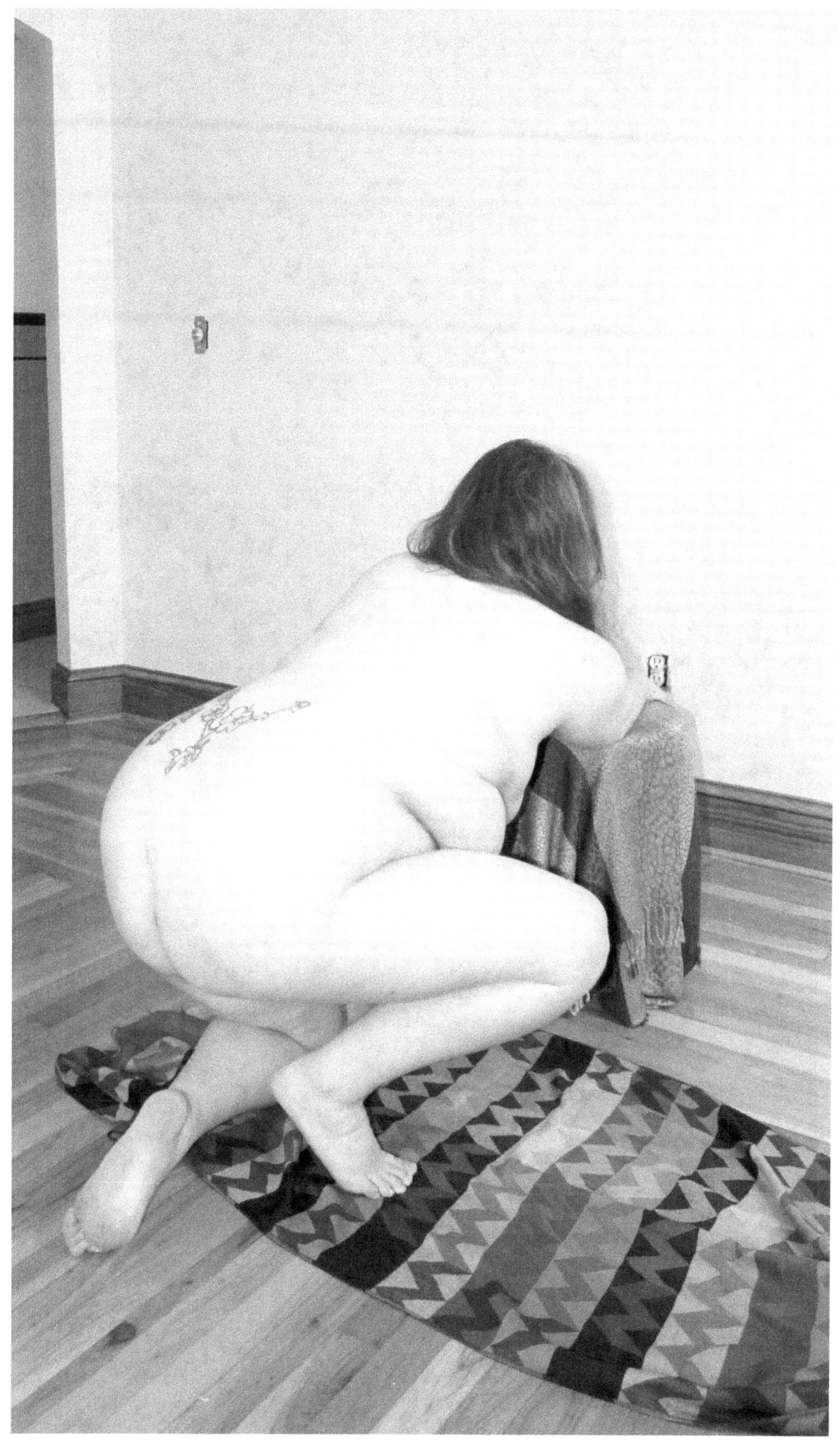

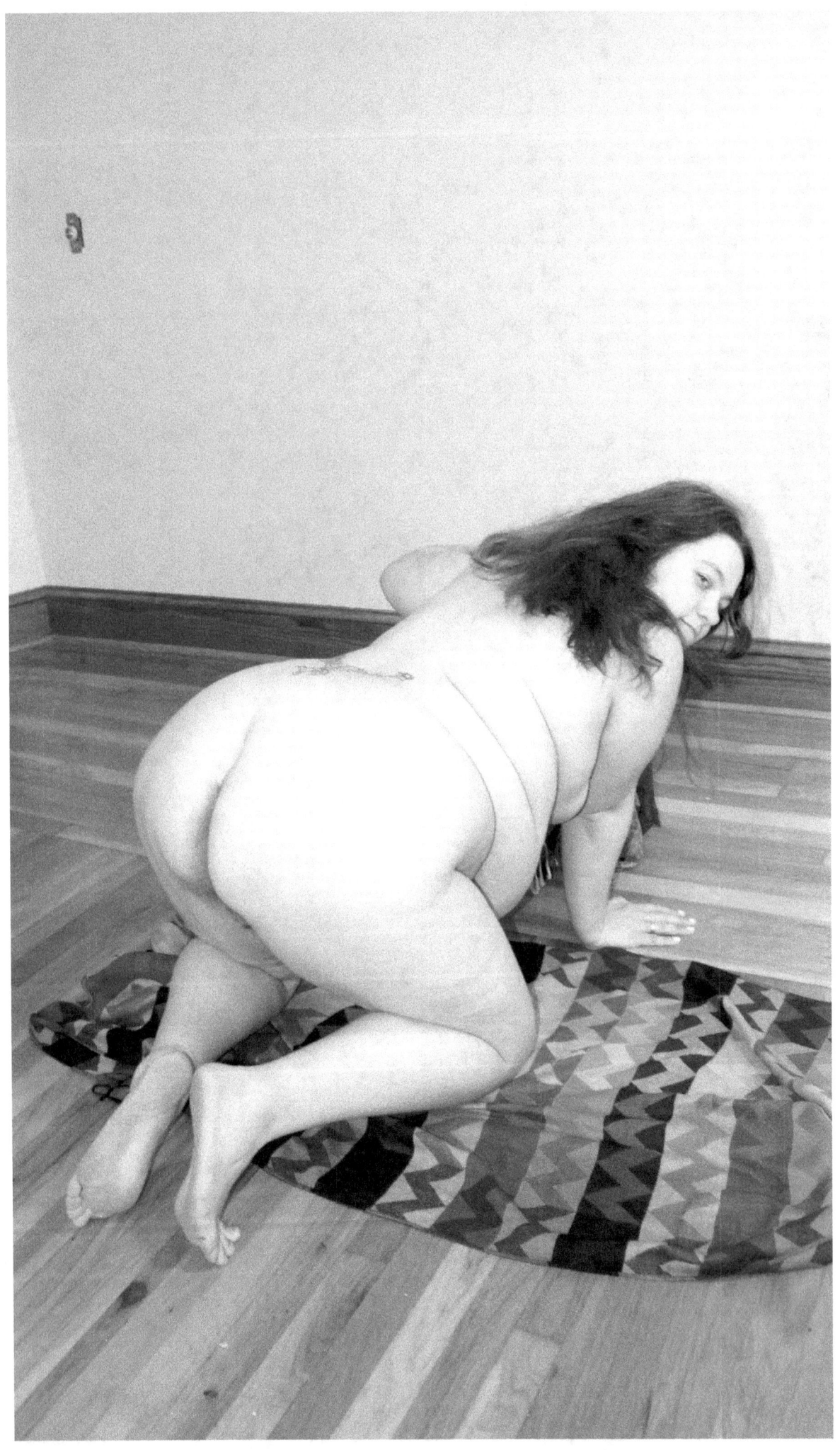

69

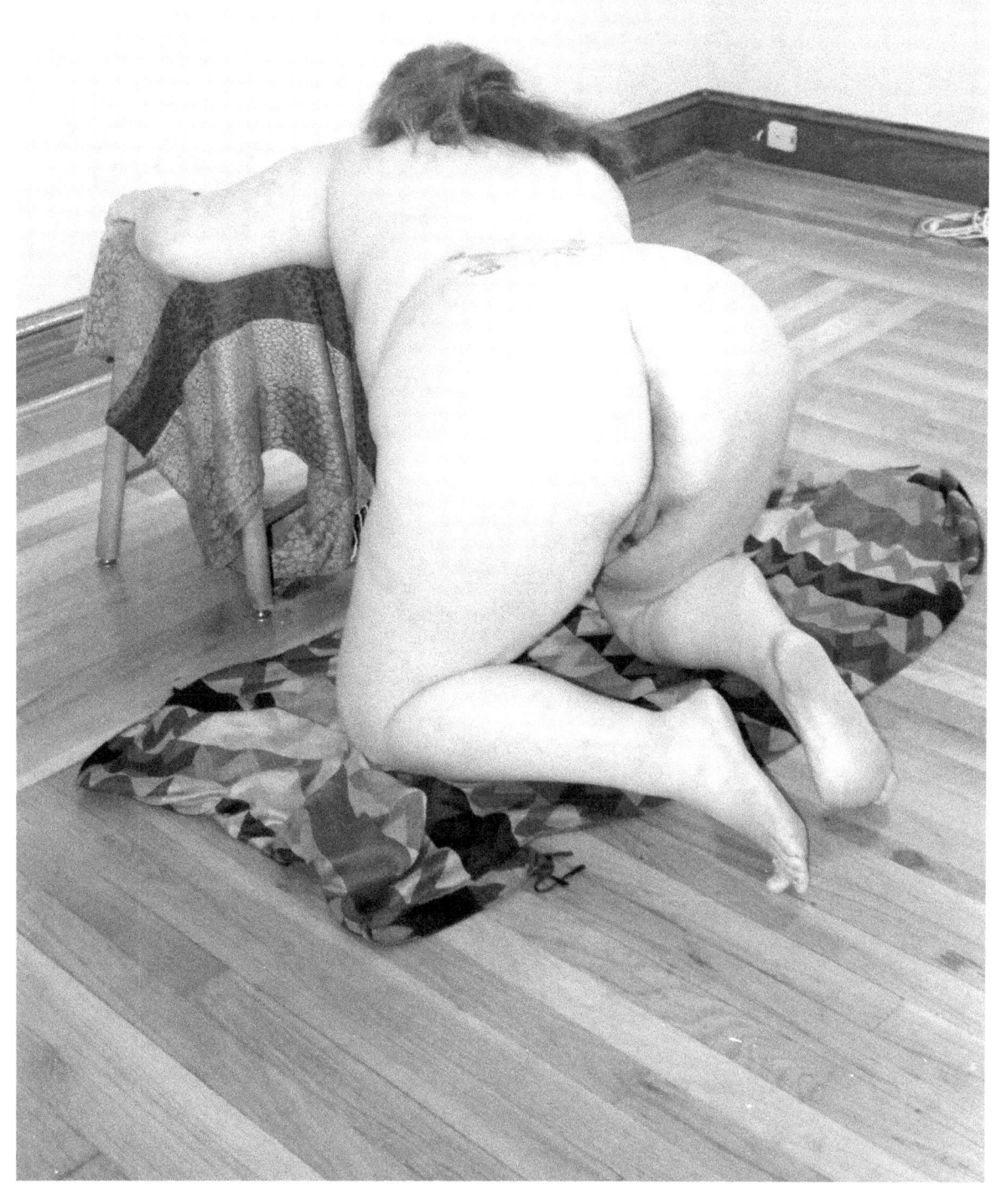

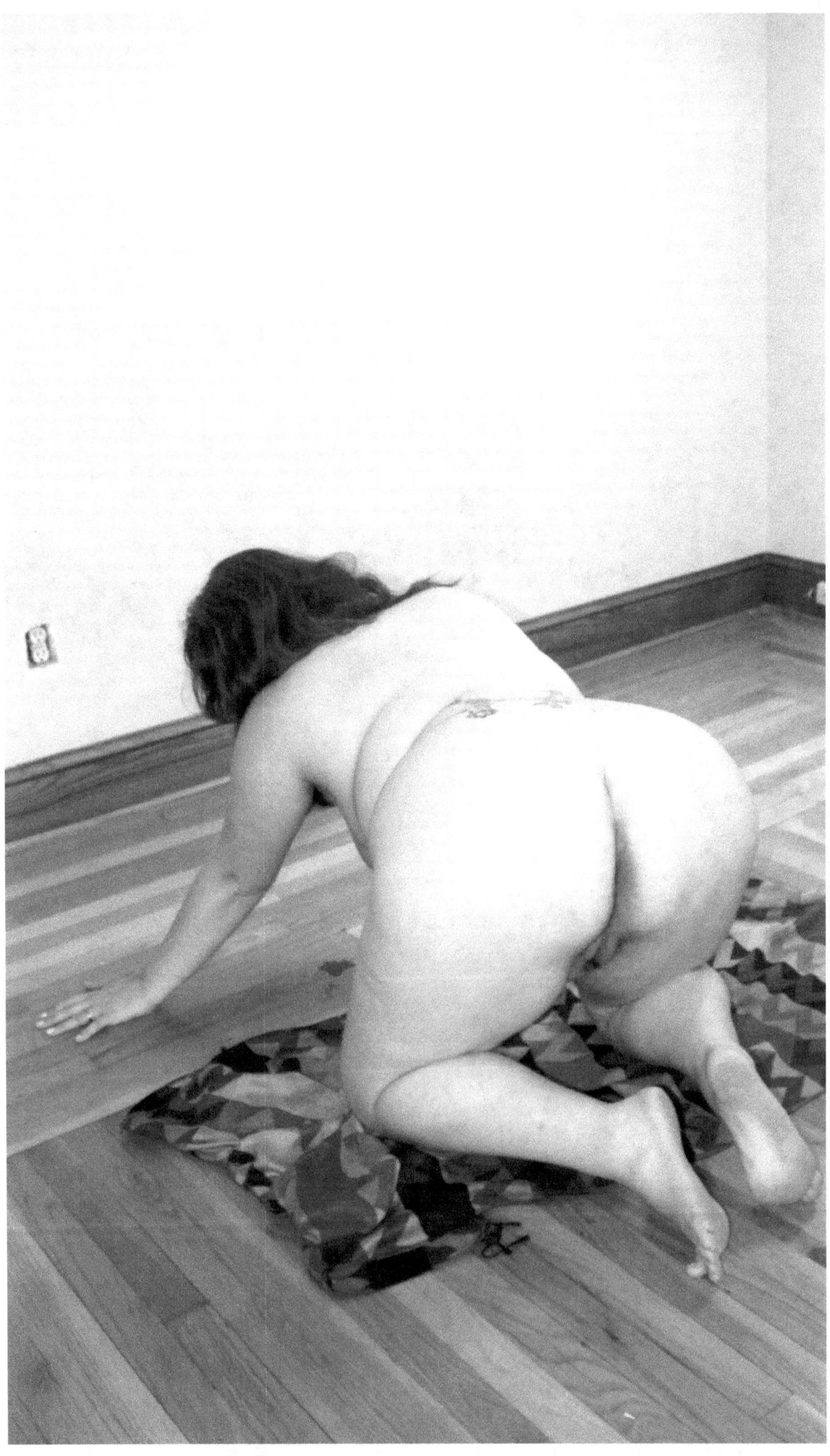

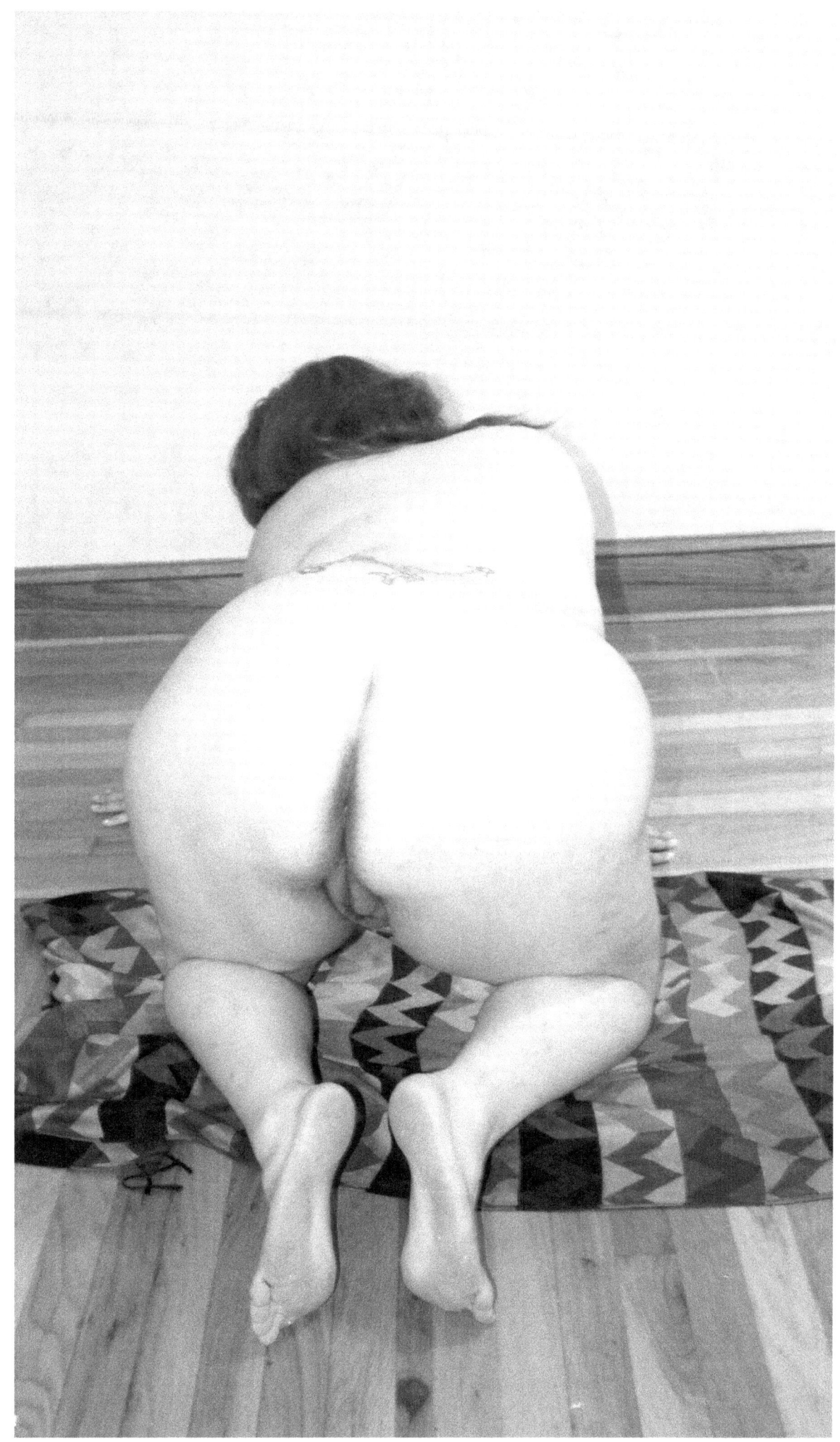

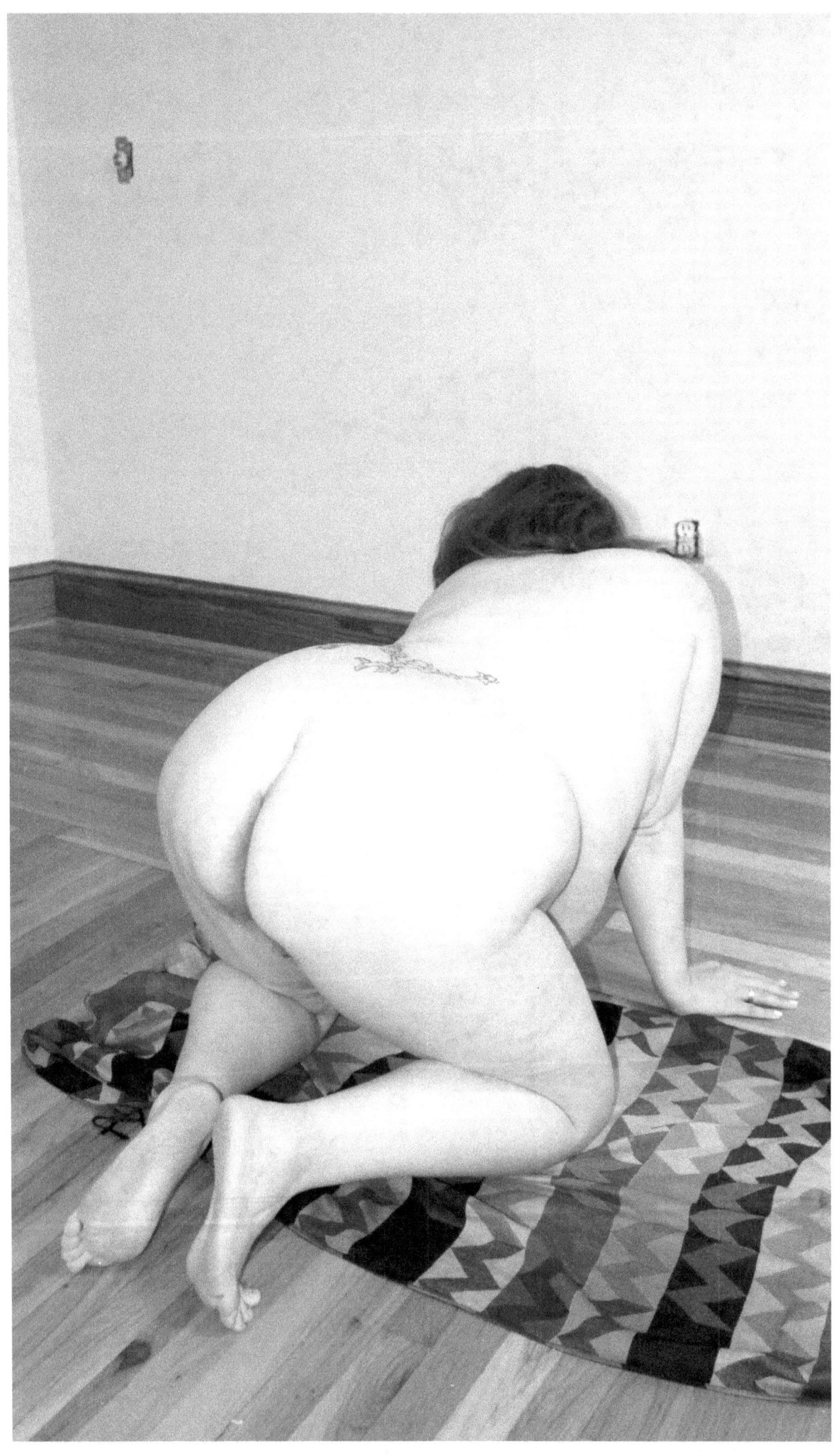

73

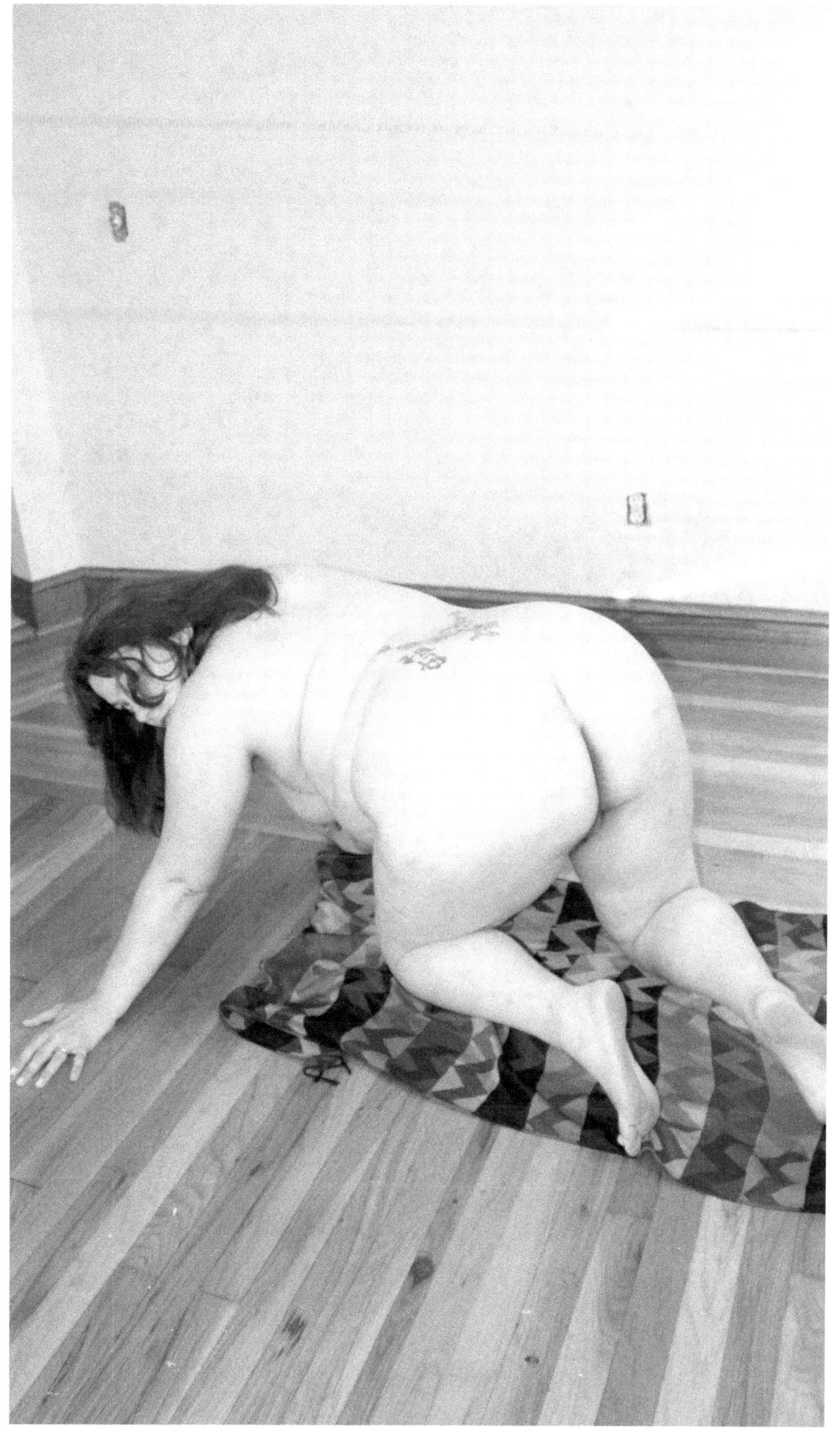

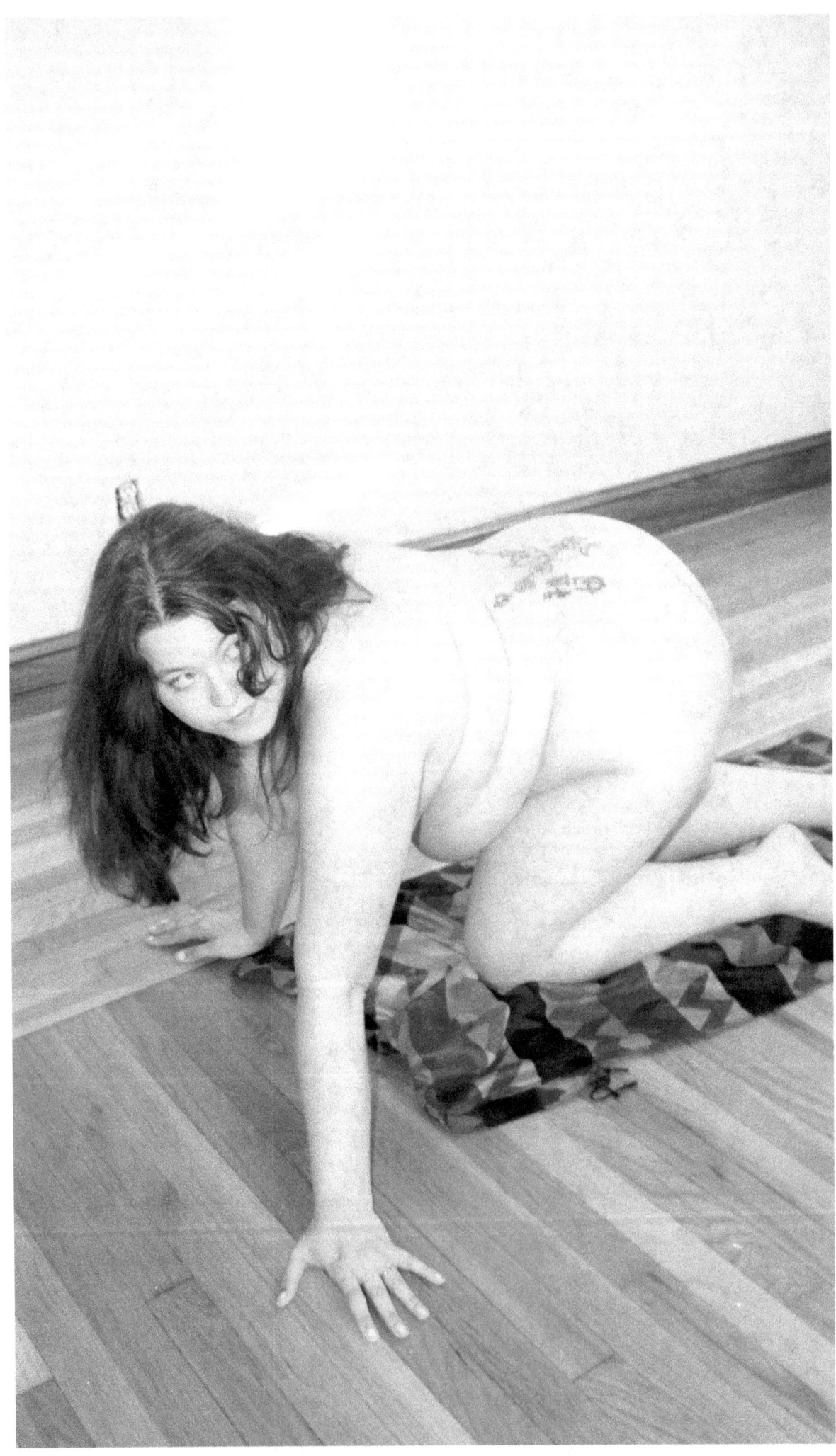

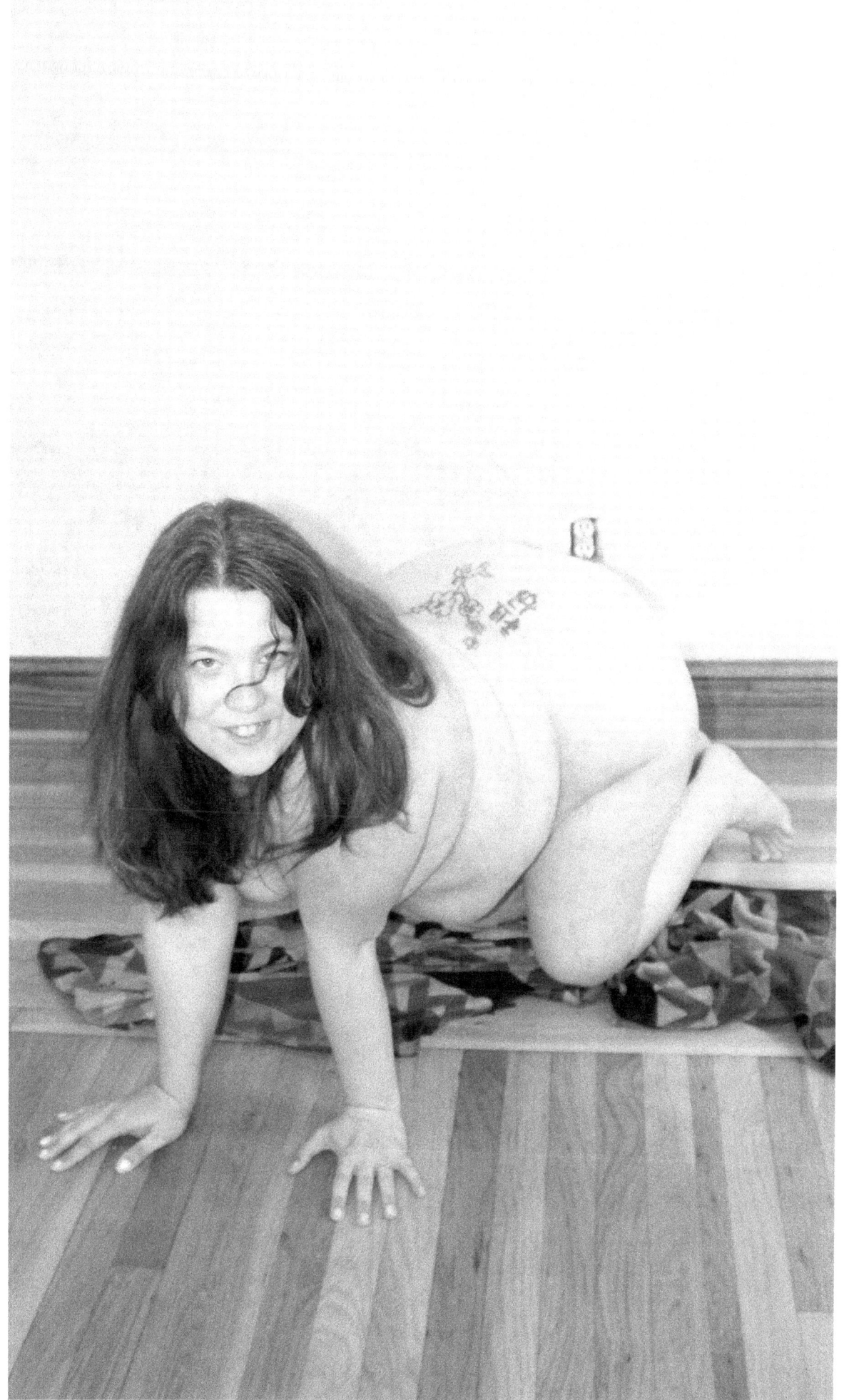

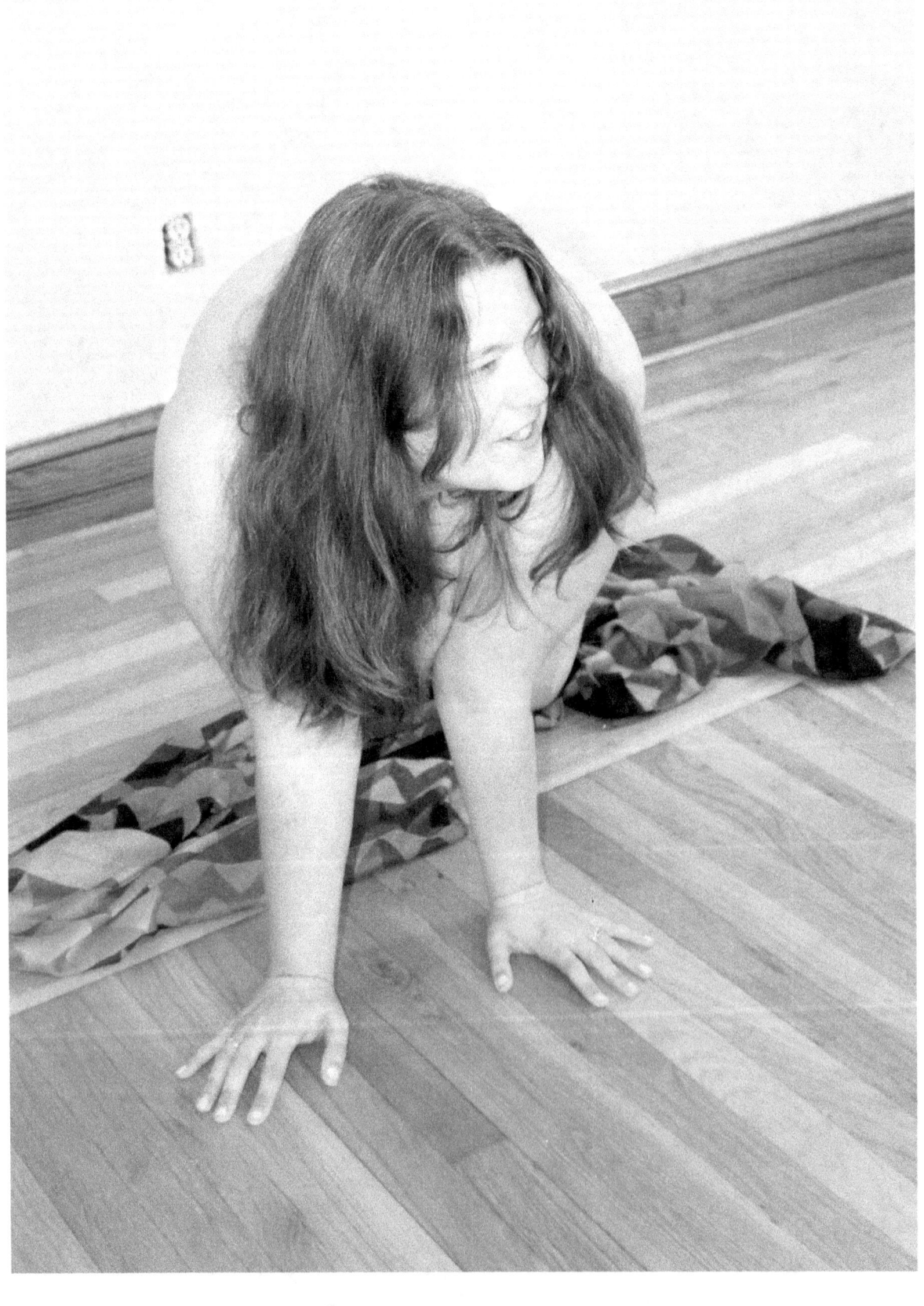

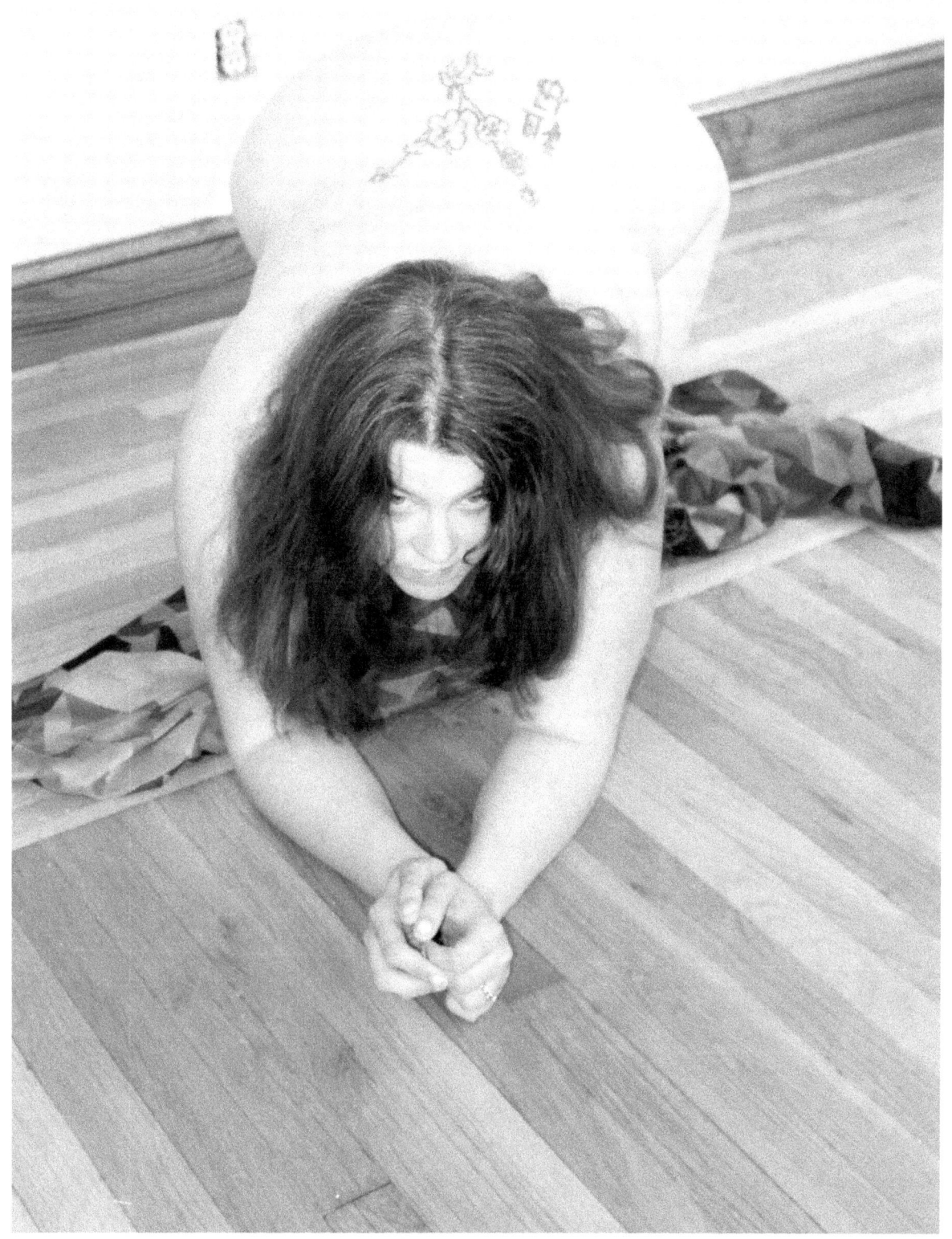

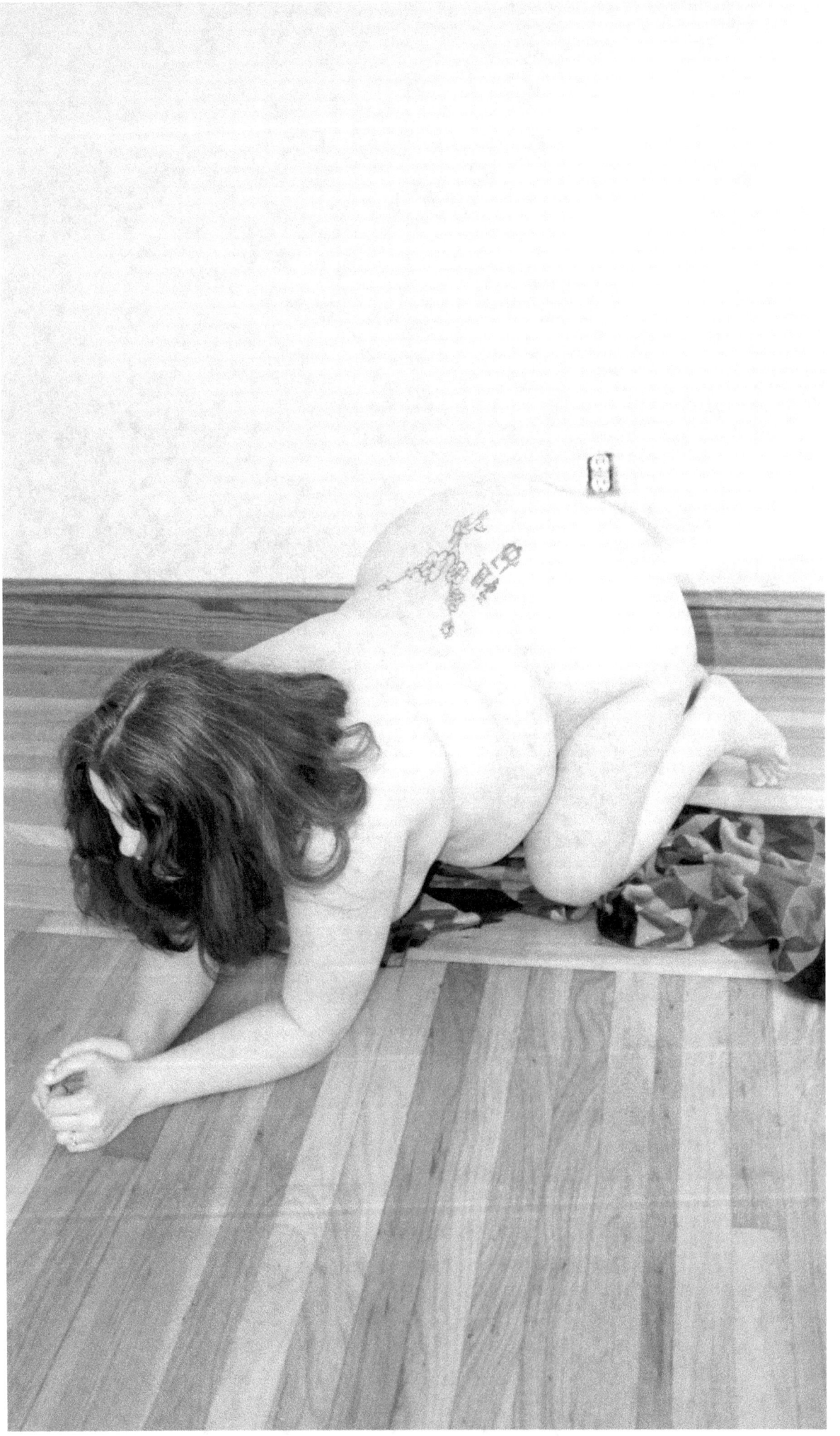

79

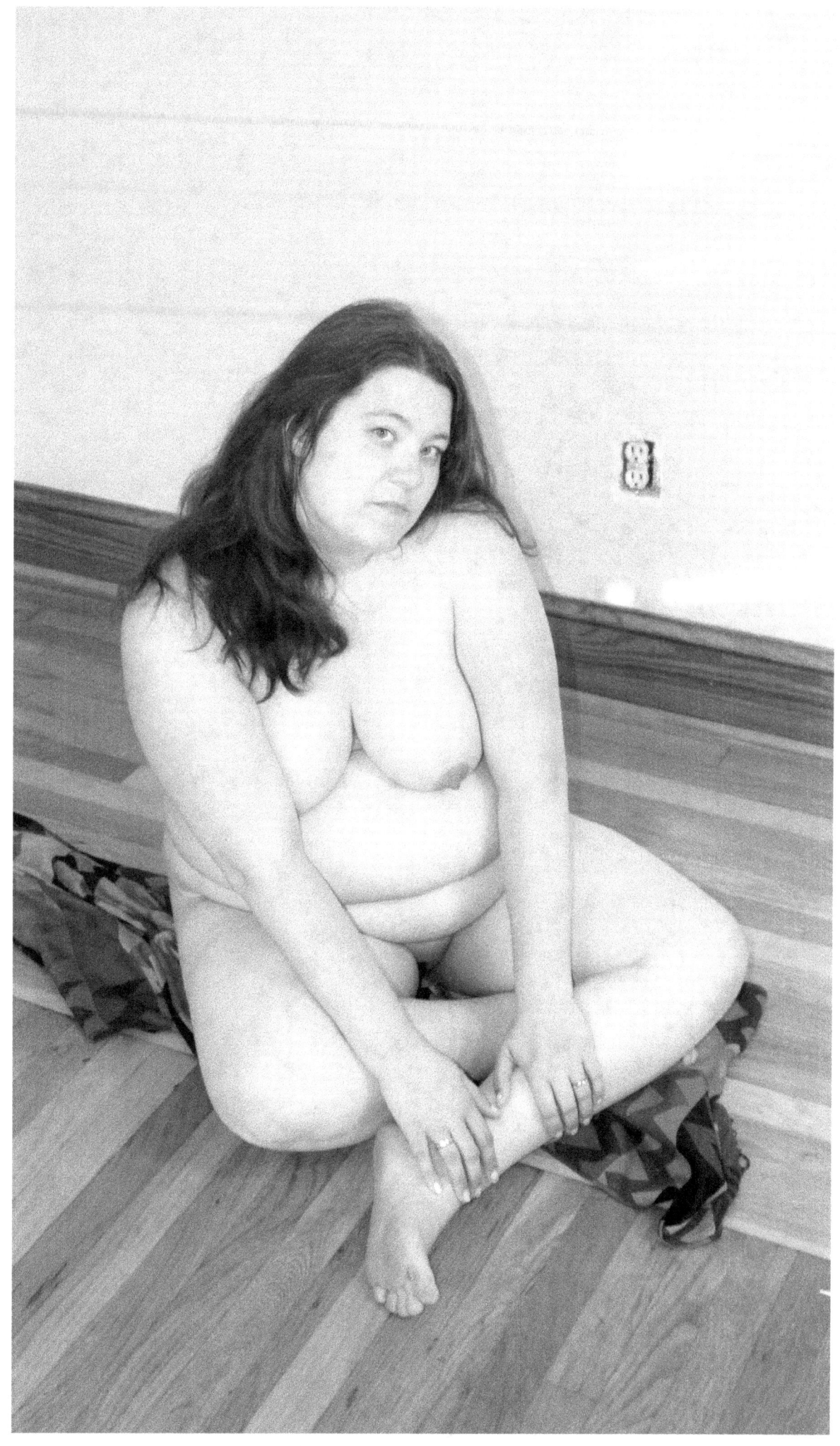

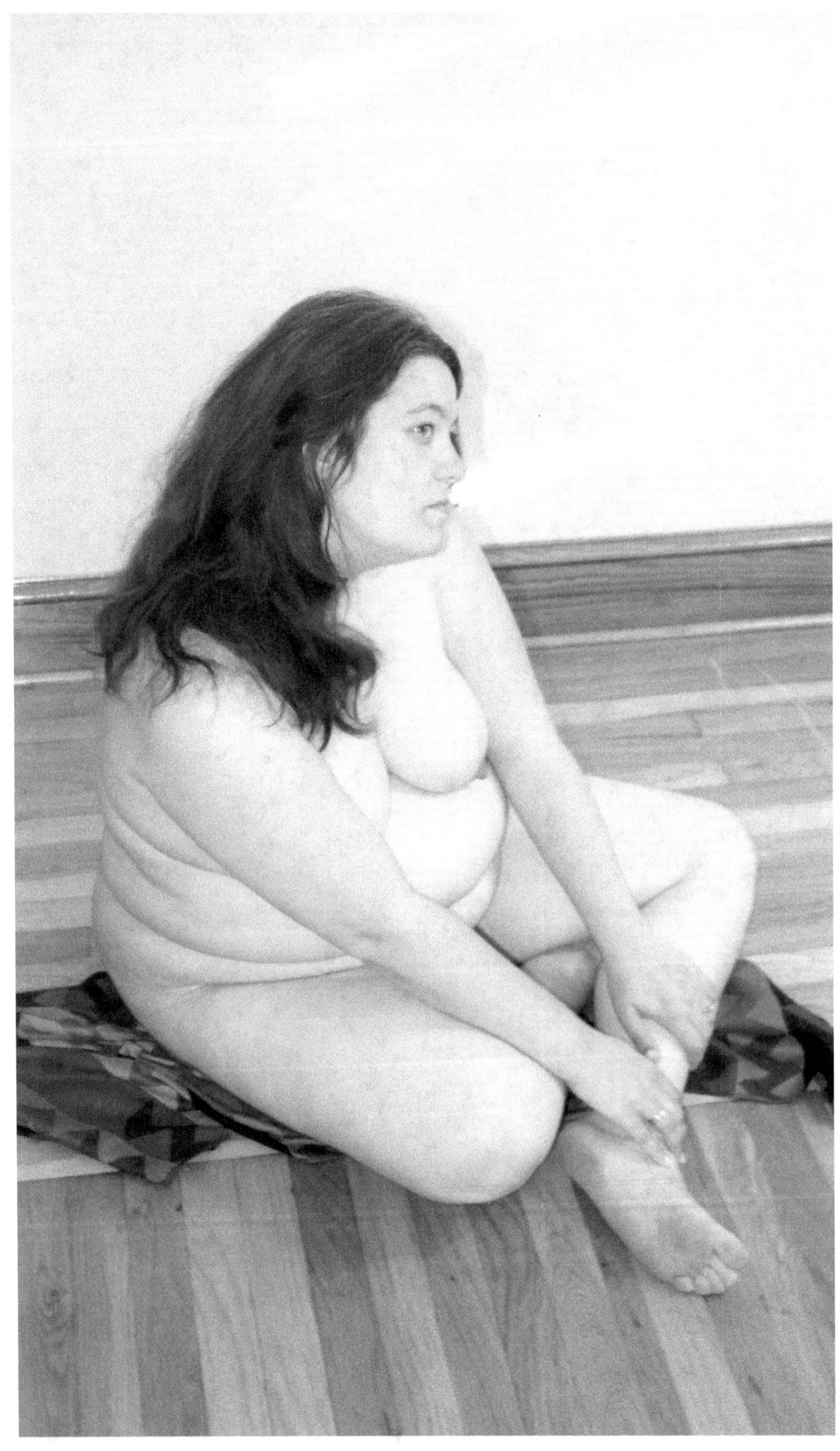

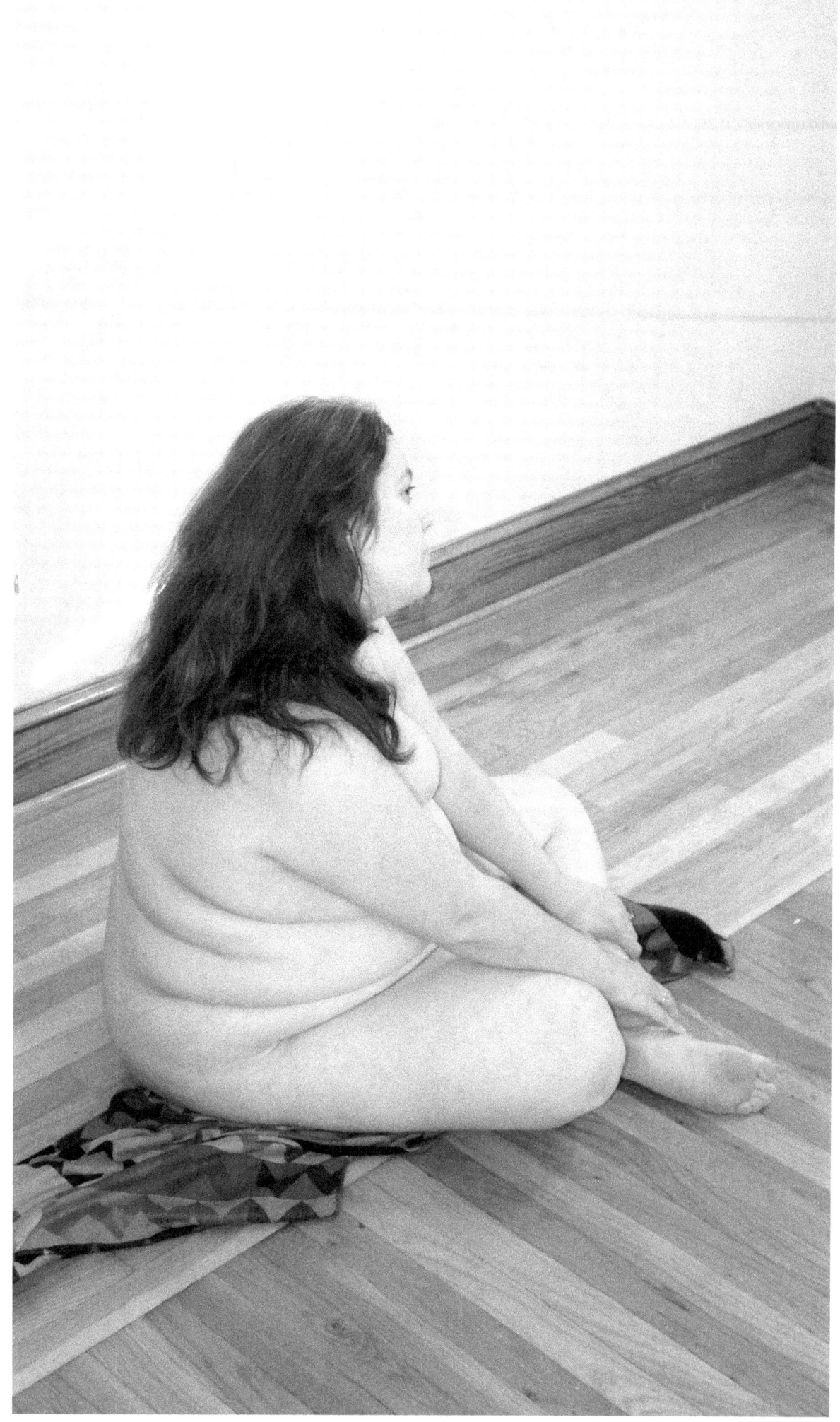

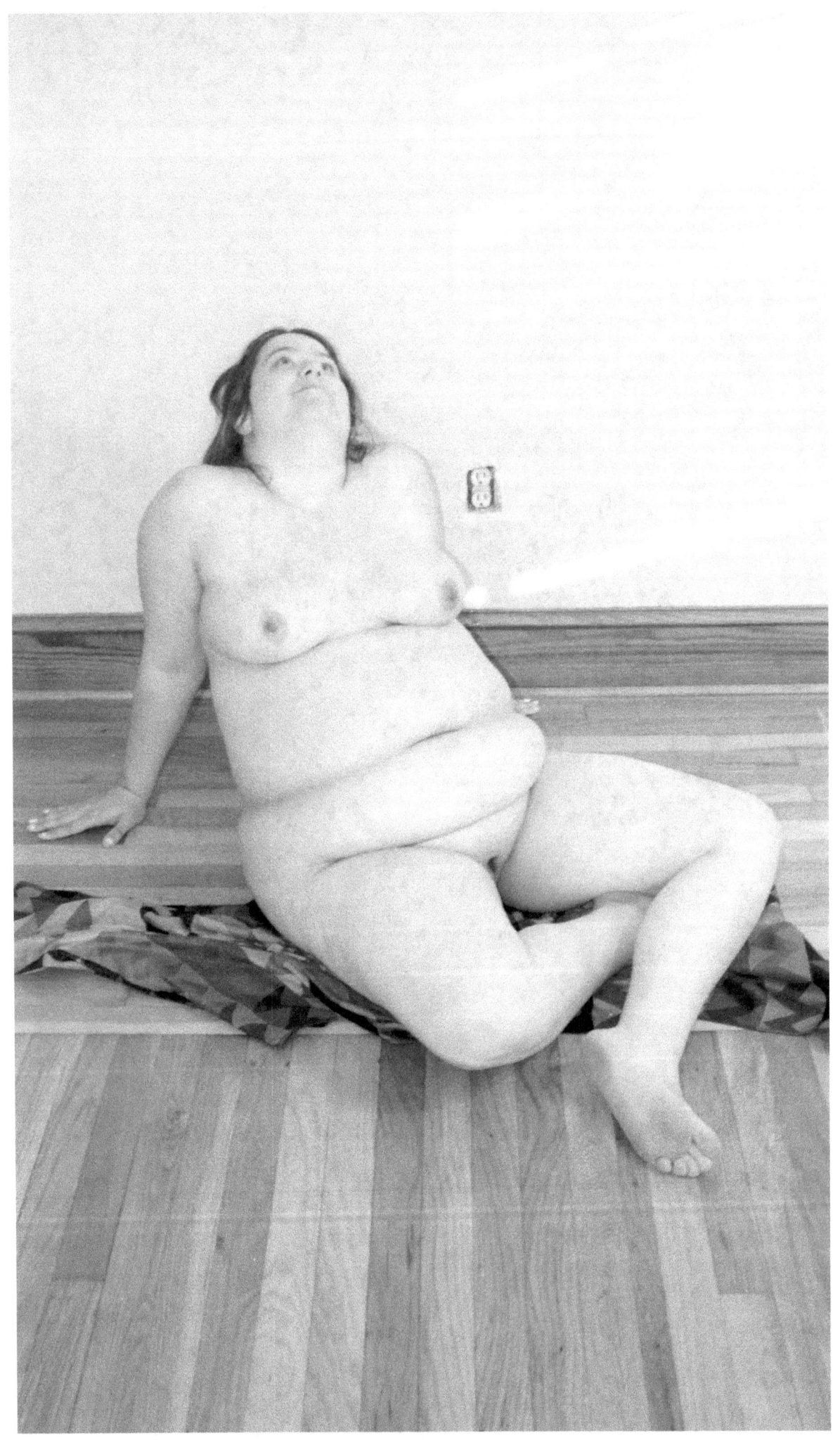

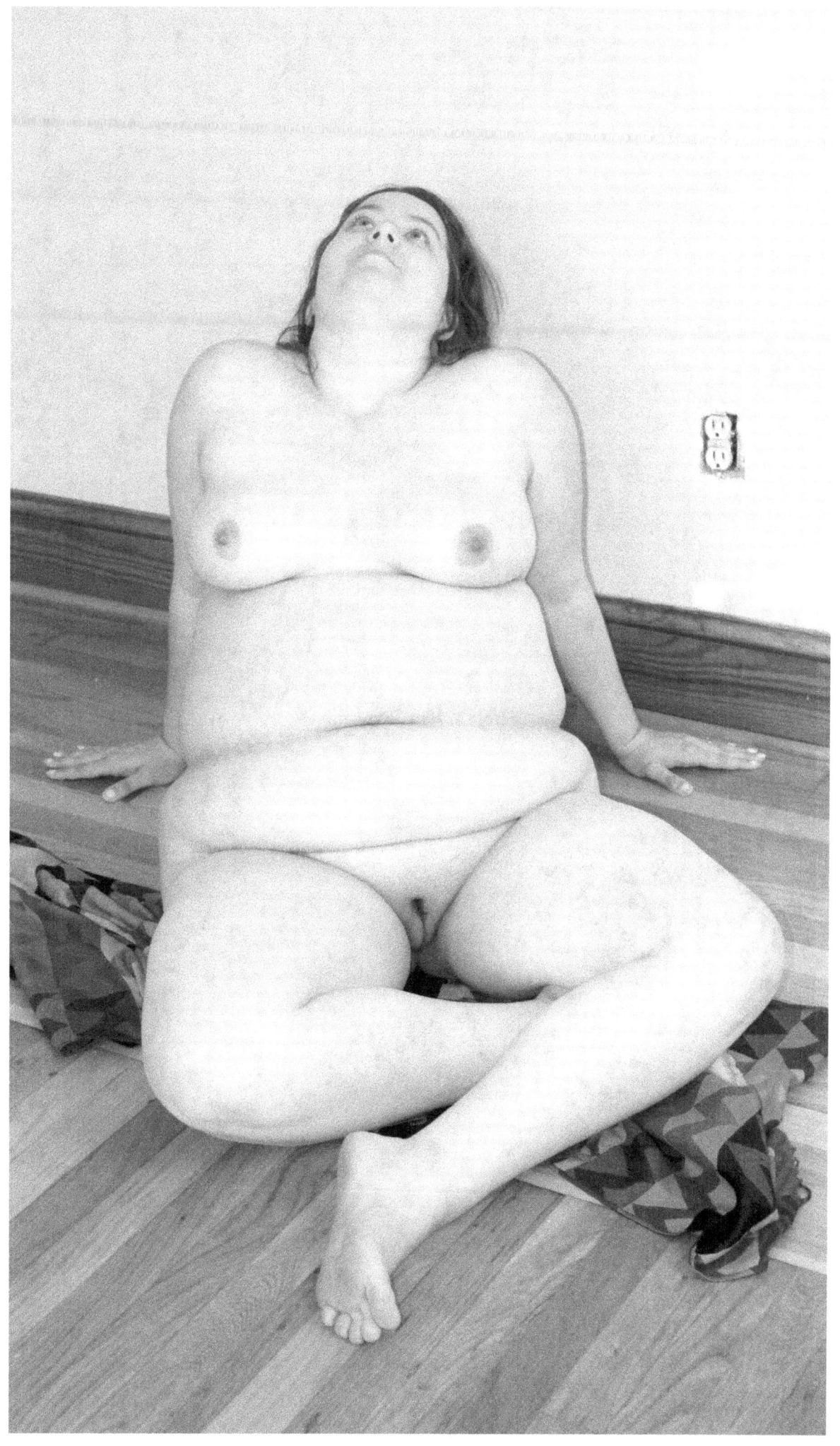

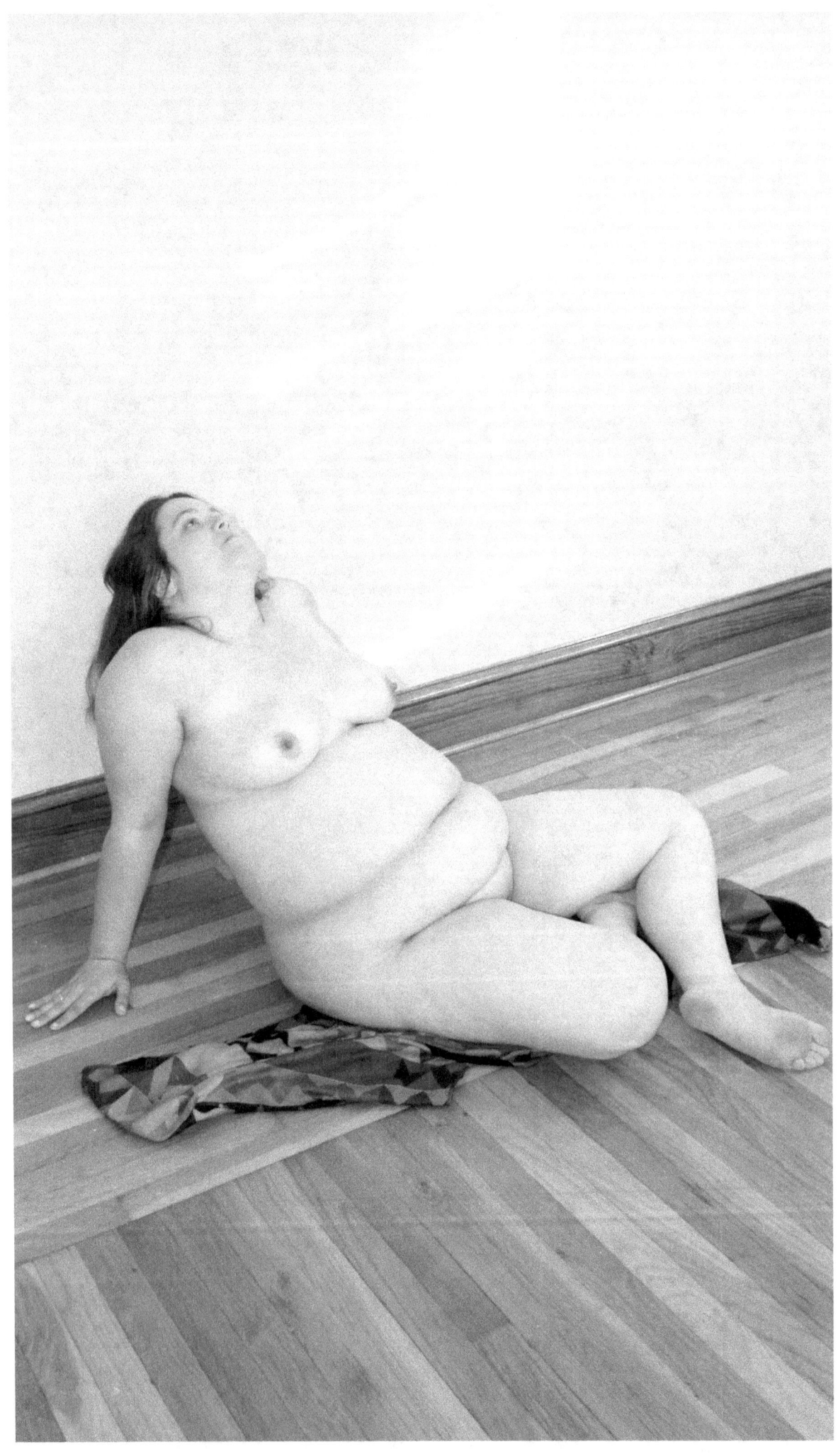

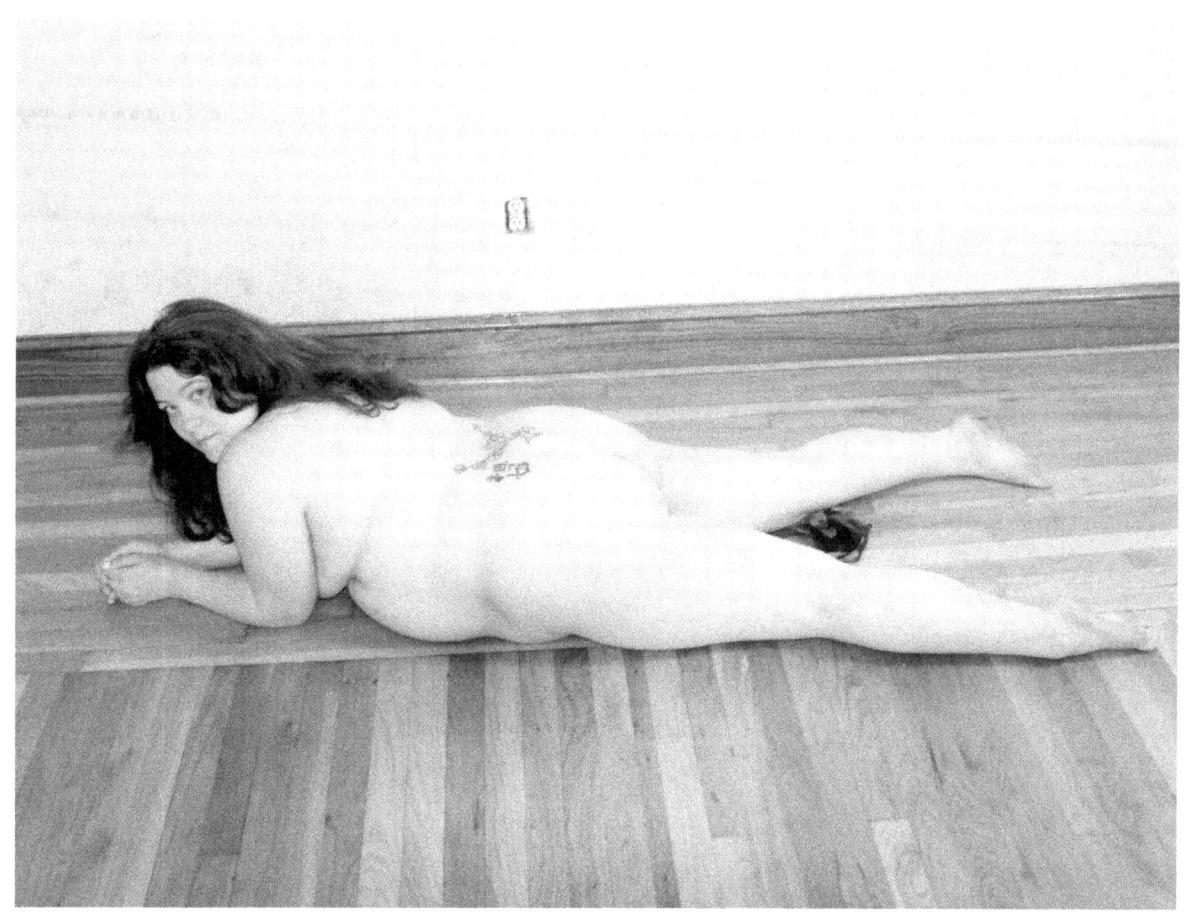

86

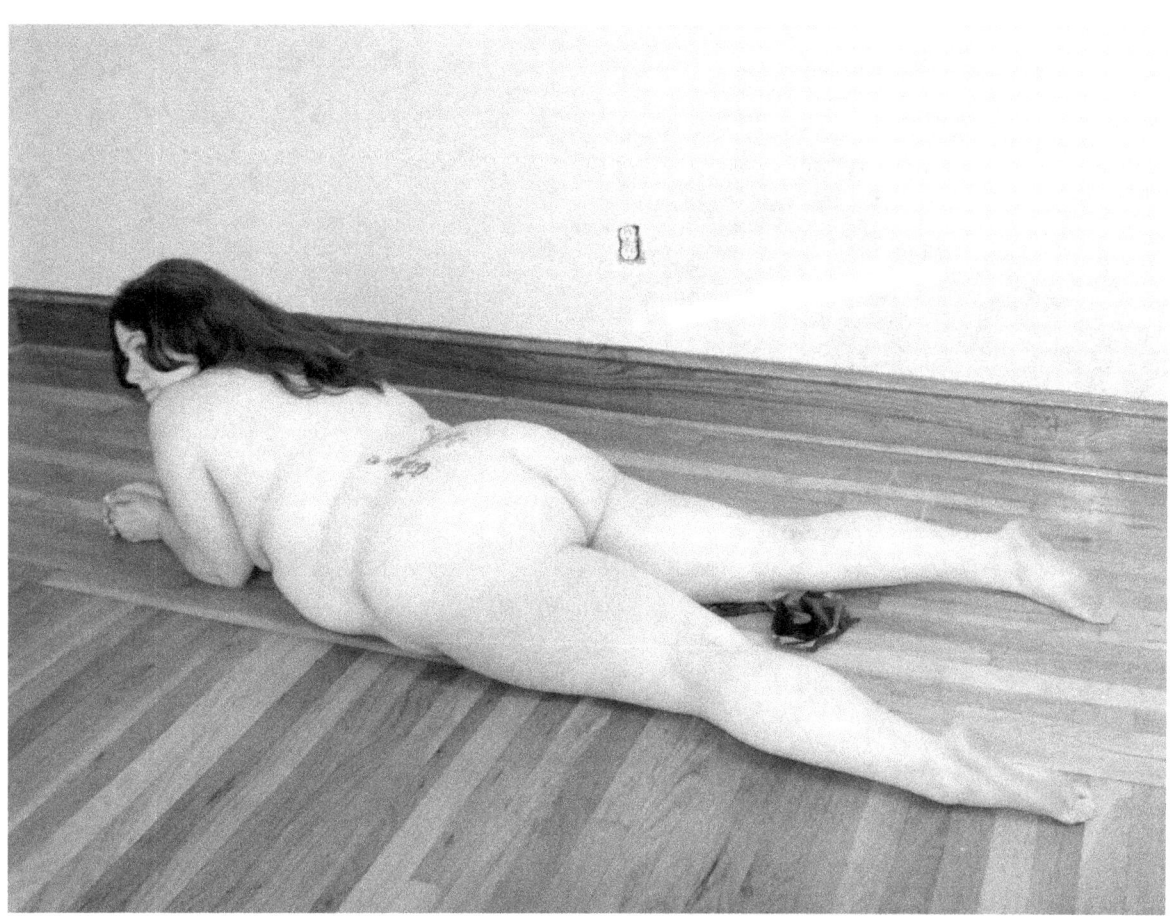

87

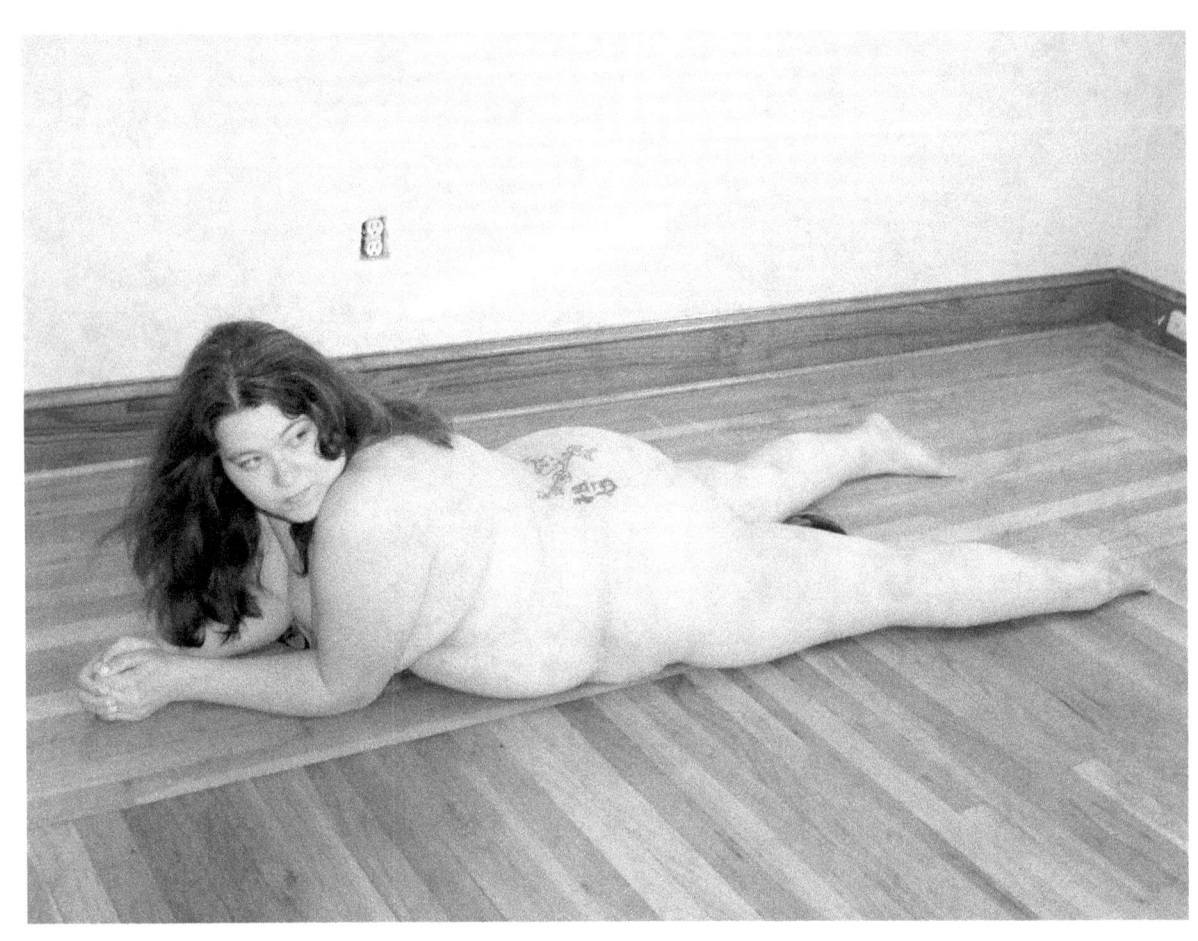

88

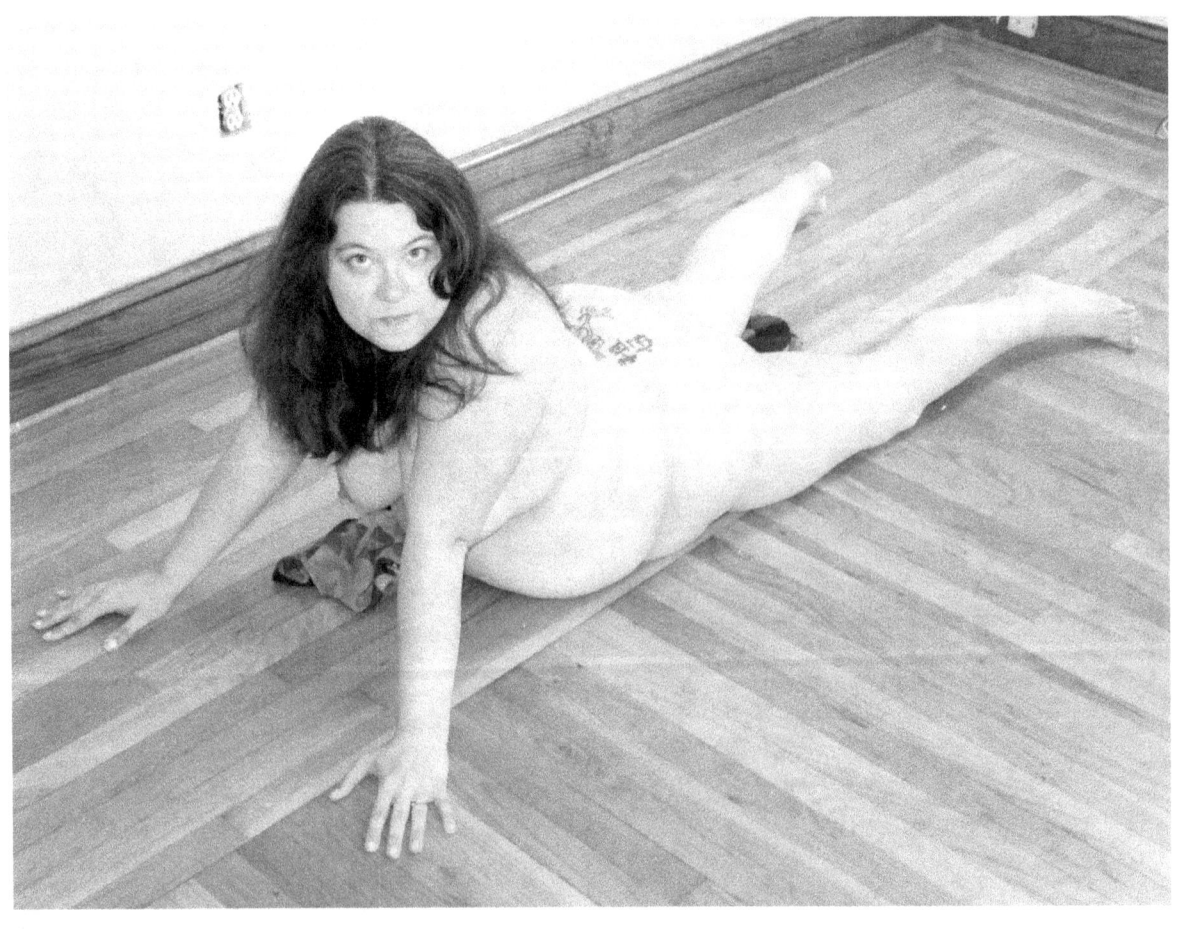

89

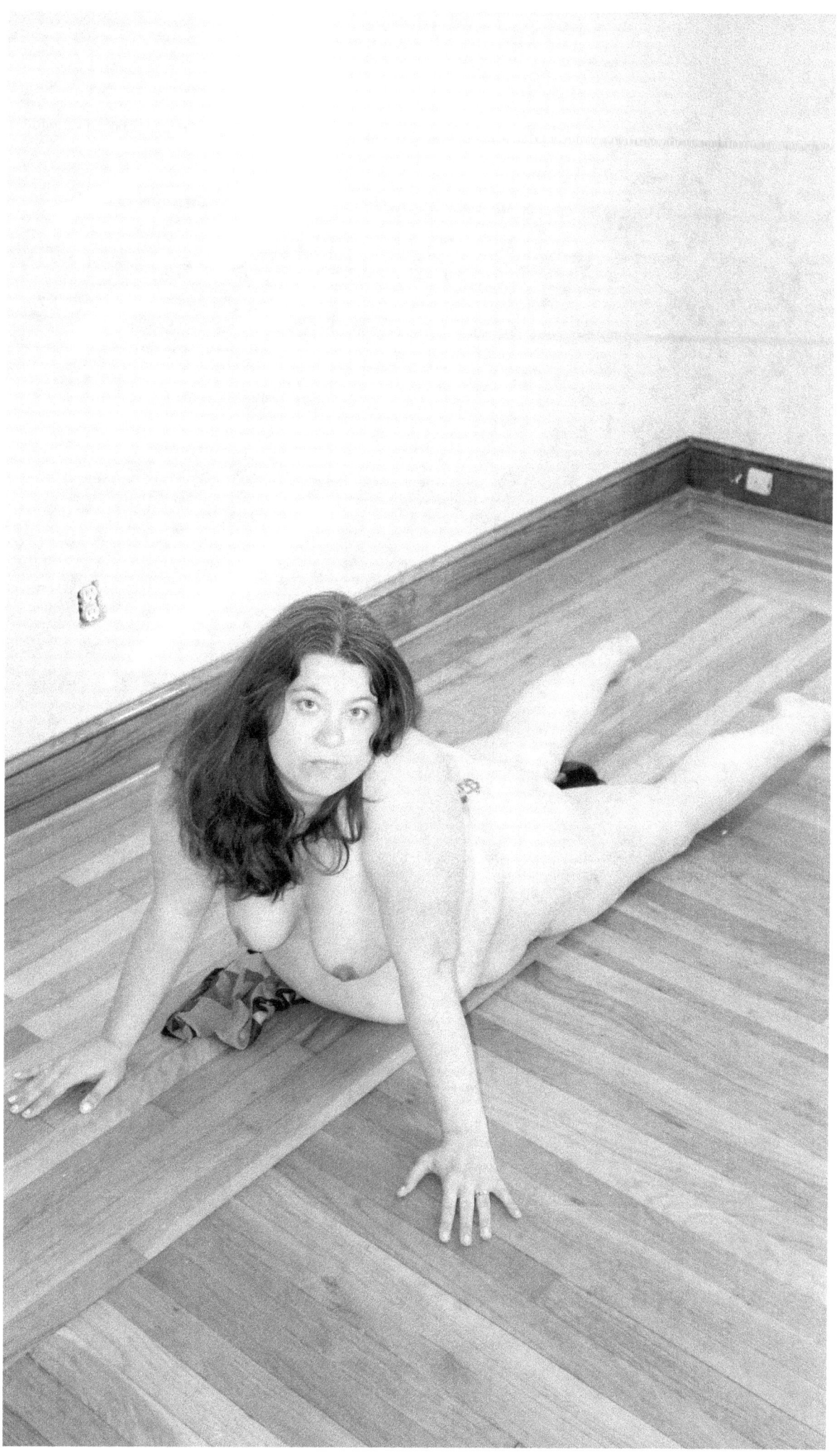

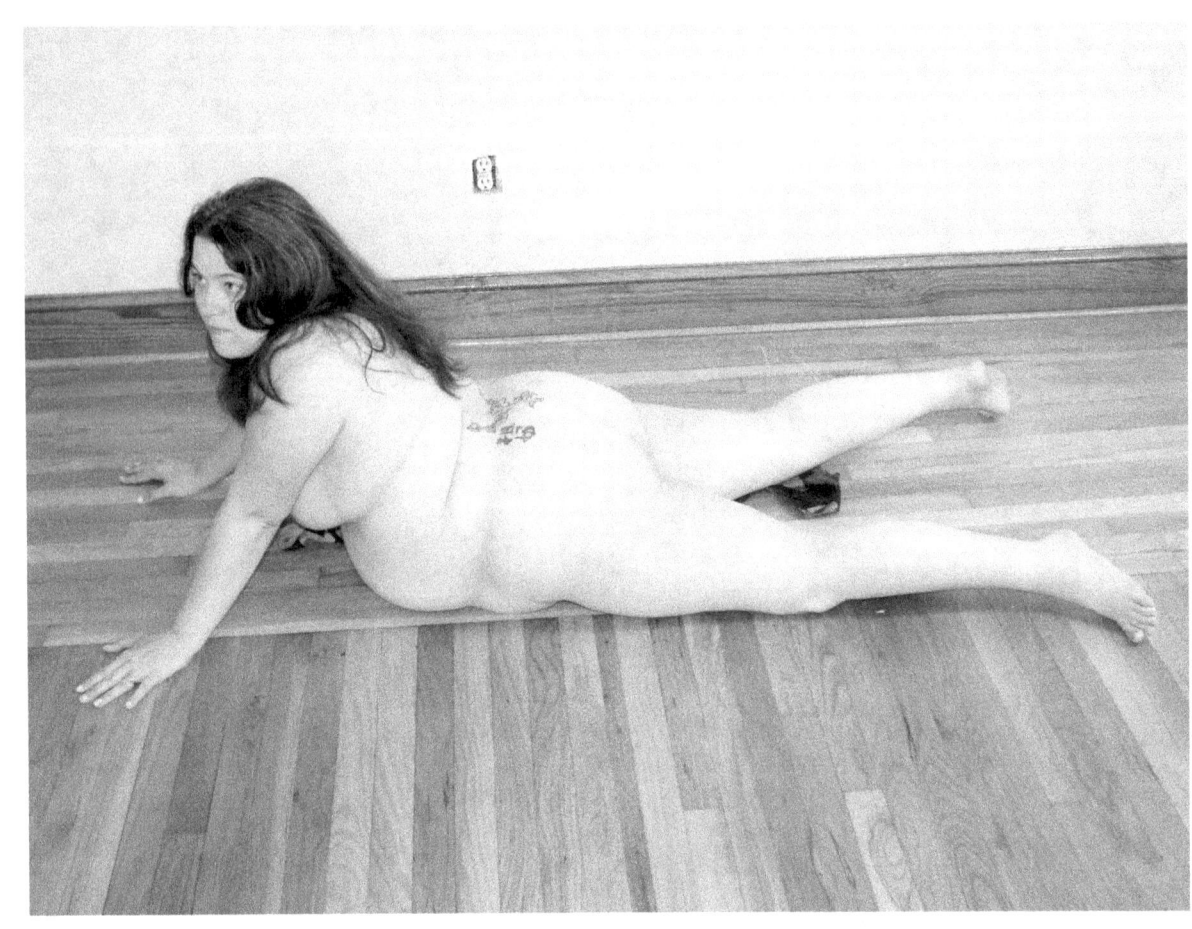

91

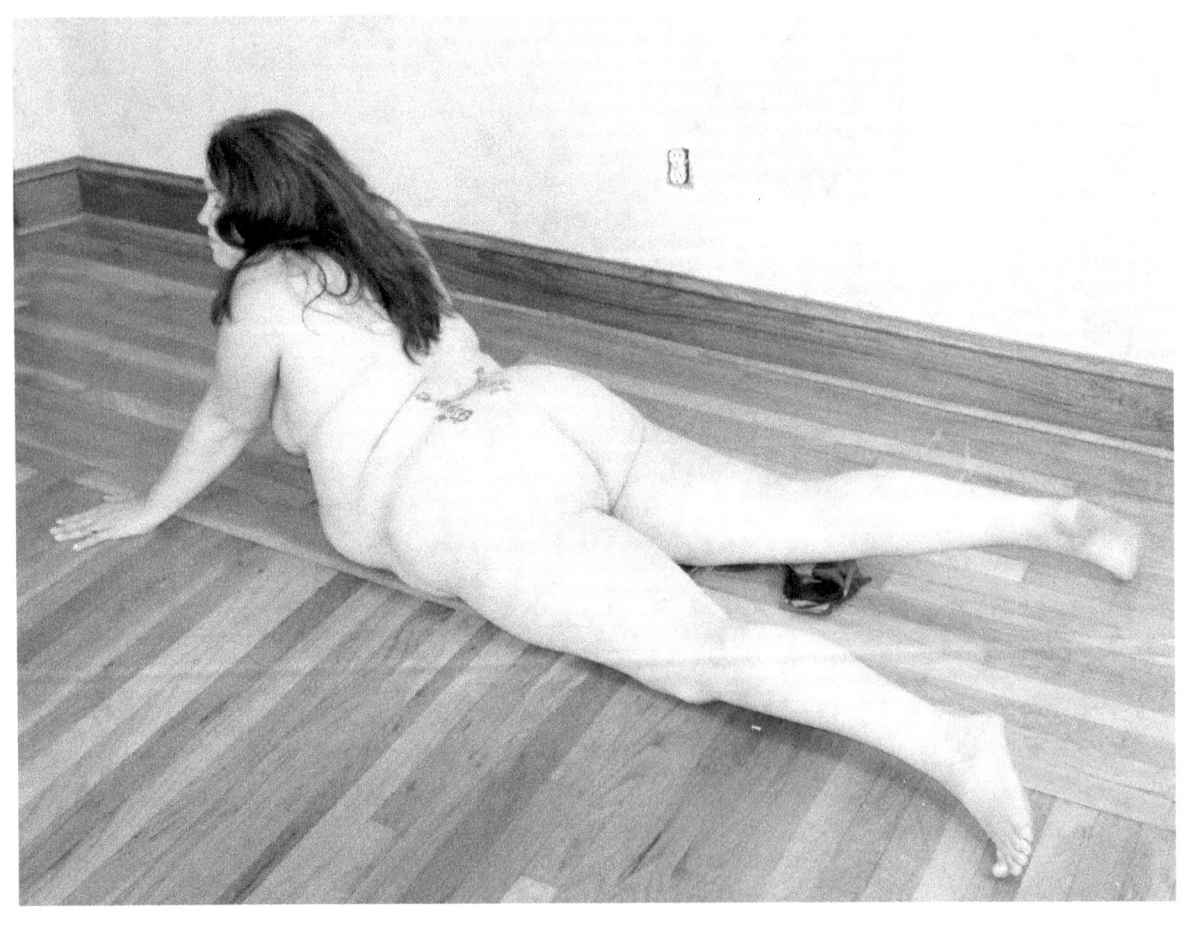

92

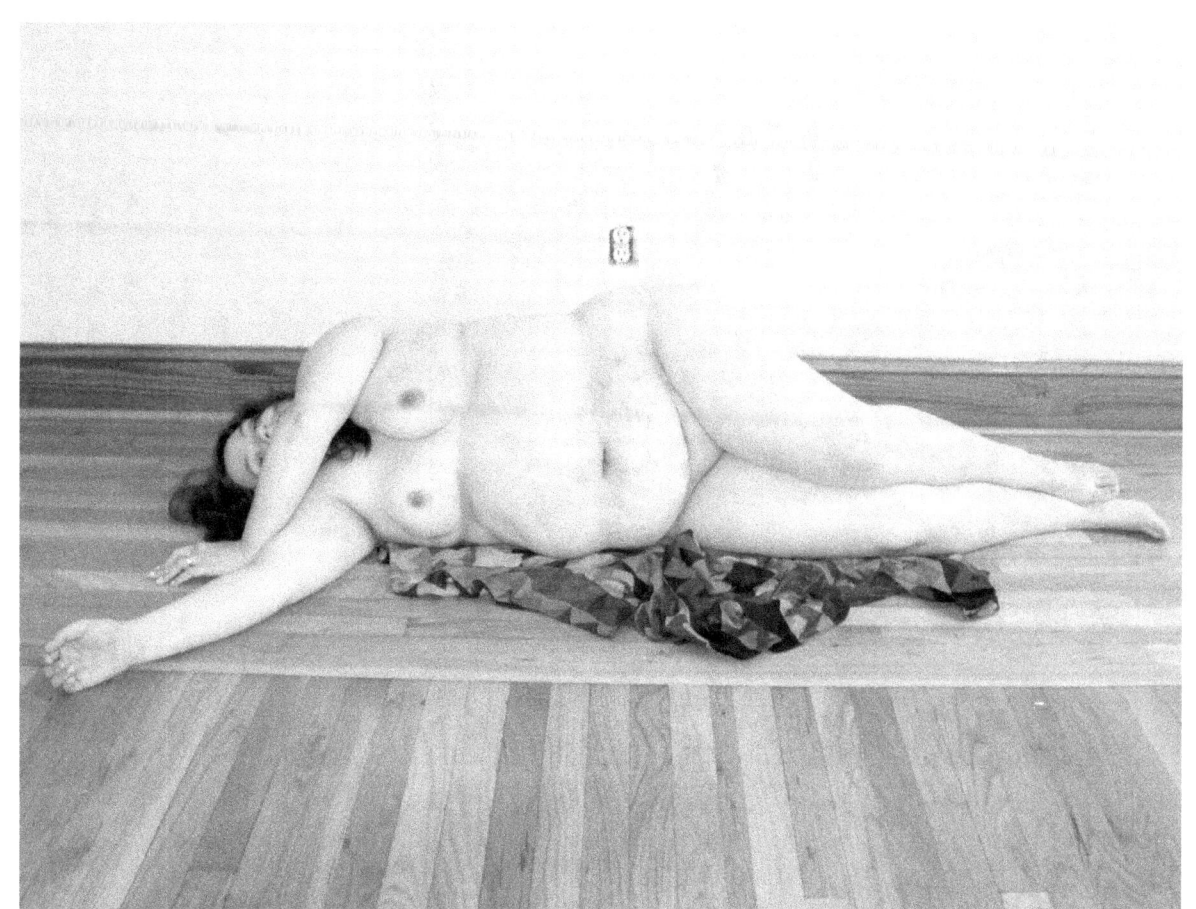

93

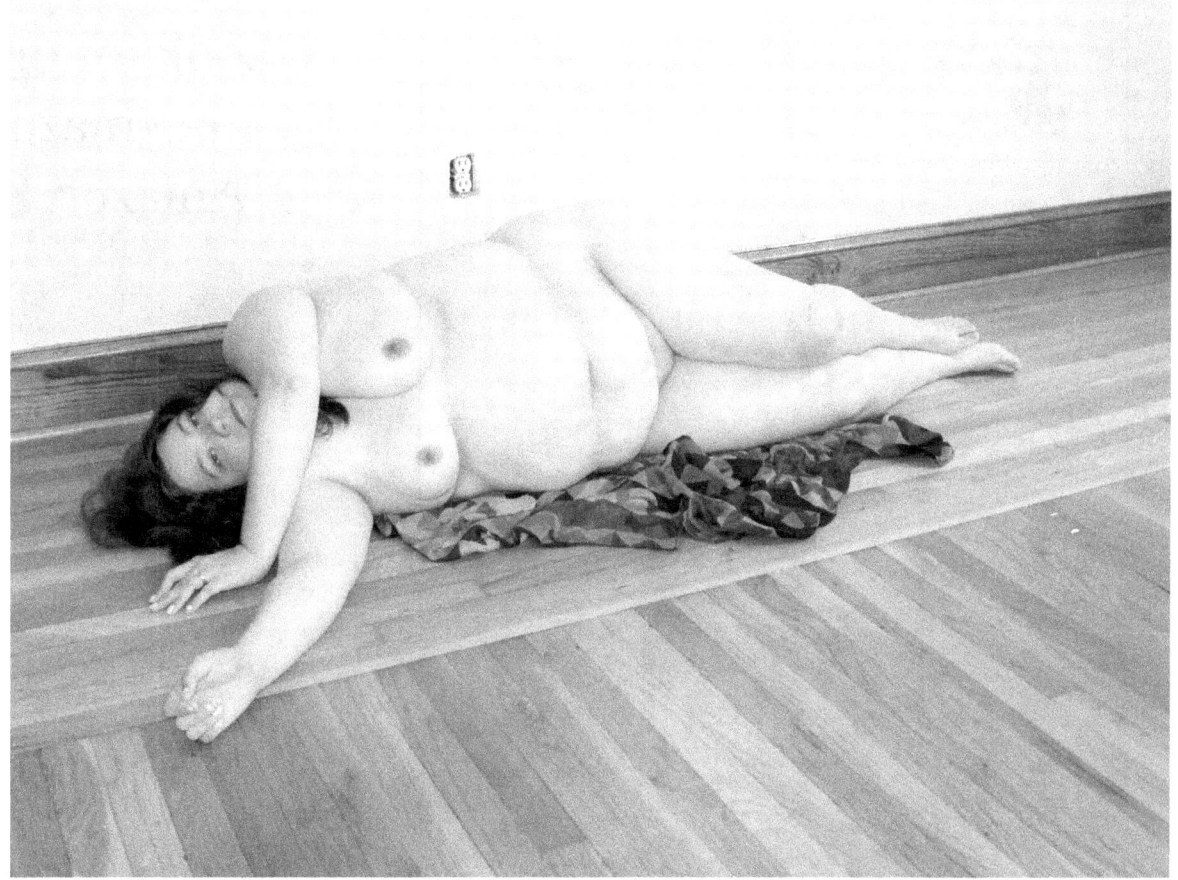

94

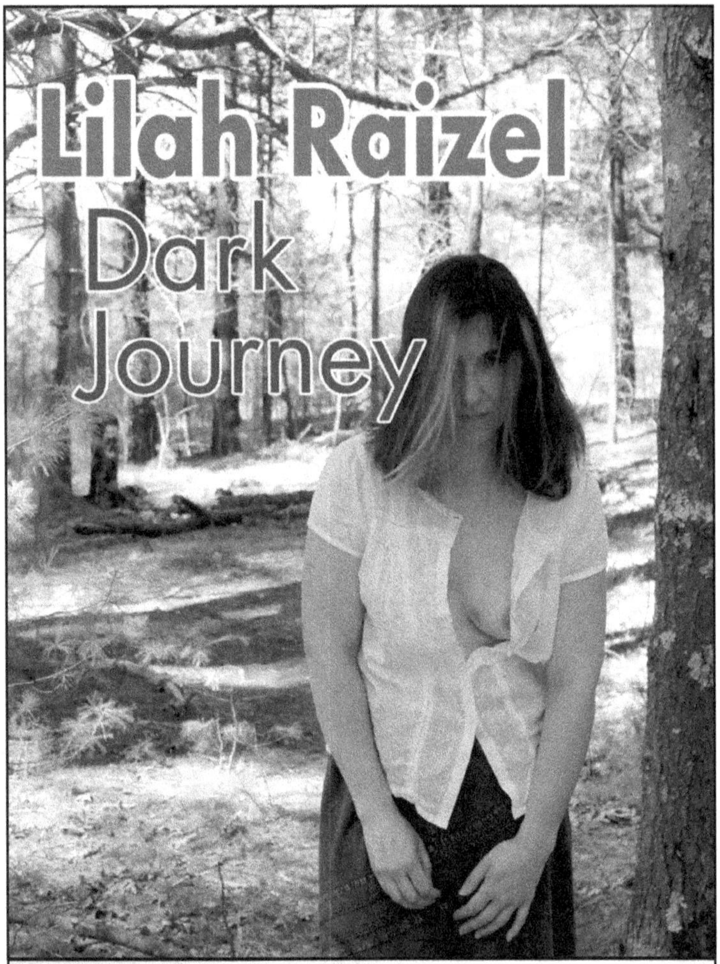

Lilah Raizel
Dark Journey

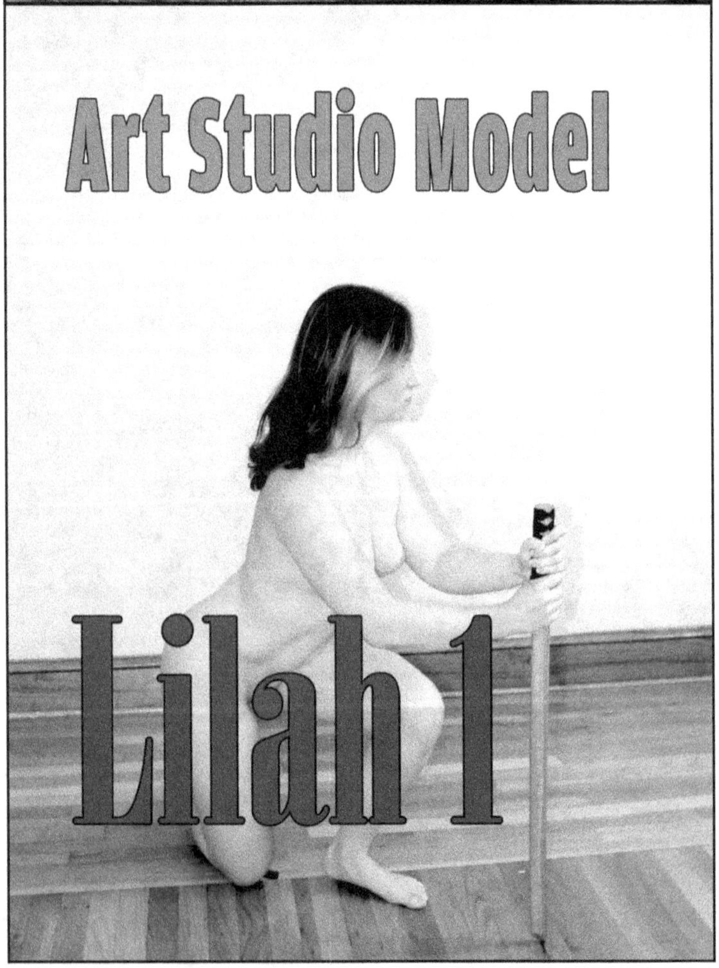

Art Studio Model

Lilah 1

Also fom
Merry Blacksmith
Studio

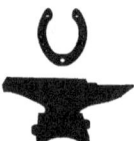

Look for our titles
on Amazon and
Amazon Kindle